TONY COLLINS

First published in Great Britain in 2016 by
The Book Guild Ltd
9 Priory Business Park
Wistow Road, Kibworth
Leicestershire, LE8 0RX
Freephone: 0800 999 2982
www.bookguild.co.uk
Email: info@bookguild.co.uk
Twitter: @bookguild

Typeset in Garamond

Images © S. Collins – T. Collins

Printed and bound in the UK by
CPI Group (UK) Ltd, Croydon, CR0 4YY

ISBN 978 1 91087 8 934

British Library Cataloguing in Publication Data.
A catalogue record for this book is available from the British Library.

FSC
www.fsc.org

MIX
Paper from
responsible sources
FSC® C013604

Dedication

This work of love is dedicated to my father, someone who has been and continues to be my friend, guide and mentor, an inspirational man of strength and loving in equal measures, supported and loved by a wonderful wife.

From a most grateful daughter: Sarita Collins. 2016.

Acknowledgements

We would like to acknowledge the co-operation and assistance provided by Danny Howell of *Solo Syndication*, Michael Pocock of the *London Evening Standard*, the *Independent* and the *Independent on Sunday*, Adam Baker of Bristol City Football Club, the Brand Protection Team at Manchester United F.C., Ruth Marsh of the *Telegraph Media Group*, Rebecca Gould of Wilson & Gould Photography, Tim Hamblin of the *Shropshire Star*, Mark of *EP Sport* and Anthony Matthews of *Newsquest* for Herts, Bucks, North and East London.

Credits

We would like to provide credit to the following list of fine journalists who reported on sporting events of the day from the early 50s to the late 80s, some of whom, when known, have been mentioned specifically within the pages of this book and others whose work may have been referred to.

1950s – Ernie Jarvis, Harold Palmer and Onlooker Columnist

1960s – Paul Doherty, Derek Wallis, Eric Thornton, Steve Haslam

1970s – Graham Russell, Herbert Gillam, Hushang Nemazee, Mike Casey, Richard Bott, Alan Thompson, Derek Potter, Simon Faber, Don Warters and Don Evans

1980s – Geoff Whitworth, Peter Godsiff, James Mossop, John Wray, David Meek and Len Noad

CONTENTS

INTRODUCTION

By

'Big Ron' Atkinson

I have known Tony Collins (TC) for many years, back to when he was Assistant Manager with Alan Dicks at Bristol City and I was manager of West Bromwich Albion. Both clubs were playing top class First Division football at a time before the Premier league, which was not introduced to English Football until February 1992. Tony was known throughout the game as a master of tactical positioning combined with shrewd assessments of players and their future potential. The team reports and dossiers he created of individual players were years ahead of anything other people were doing. He had a knack of spotting very young players with good ingredients and potential playing in amateur leagues or reserve teams of professional clubs. Tony considered they were not being given the opportunity to showcase their natural talents in the first team, and he also knew how to put a price on the 'big hitters'.

Tony became a talent spotter of unrivalled proportions after many successful playing years with Sheffield Wednesday, York City, Crystal Palace, Watford, Norwich City, Torquay United and a managerial career starting as Player/Manager at Rochdale. He had a track record with Rochdale and Bristol City of either obtaining a player very cheaply, or on free transfer; the likes of Geoff Merrick, Gerry Gow, Paul Cheesley, Trevor Tainton and Tom Ritchie for Bristol City. One other memorable coup that comes to mind is the signing of Gordon McQueen for Leeds United. Tony was instrumental in moving

Norman Hunter to Bristol City and the controversial capture of Lee Sharpe for Manchester United.

I had no hesitation in appointing him my Chief Scout at Manchester United with the main reason being he was part and parcel of the reason for Don Revie's success with the great Leeds United team, which was the best team in the land by a mile at that time. It was well known he was Don's right hand man not only for talent spotting, but for his in depth analysis of opposition tactical play, particularly in Europe. He went on to become one of the best known names in the boardrooms of many of the major clubs of the day, as well as the English national side under Don Revie. He made headline news on all the sports pages and was given a testimonial match at Bristol City in 1977 against an all England eleven with England manager Ron Greenwood turning up to take charge of his team and Elton John taking the kick off!

This is not only the story of a man's life devoted to football, it's also a story of overcoming prejudice and discrimination to become Norwich City's and Crystal Palace's first black player, the first black manager in the English football League, and to be the manager of the only 4th division club to ever get to the league cup final with Rochdale. I therefore hope you enjoy this fascinating and well written biography of a man who has entered his 90th year and devoted most of those years to a sport we all love.

Ron Atkinson.

WHO WAS TONY COLLINS – MASTER SPY?

That's the question, so what is the answer? Well, if you were around in the 60's and 70's and had more than a passing interest in English football, you would know. Showbiz celebrities of the time, such as Elton John and Pat Phoenix certainly did. His name was all over the National press sports pages, and for all the right reasons. This is the extraordinary story of a singularly remarkable man. The telling of it will fascinate football fans, for it describes the life of a man hailed as one of the early pioneers of the 'beautiful game' … played intelligently. It will also provide a new insight into a particular social chronicle of the time.

Tony Collins was a child of mixed parentage but to the rest of the world, at that time in our history, it would be irresistible to not regard him as a black man. Of course, there were many social complications of the day to contend with. For example, after the 1939–1945 war, rationing was maintained in the UK for some years. The now famous signs also began appearing in some boarding house windows showing the owners preference for 'No Dogs, No Blacks, No Irish'. Memories of the days between the wars, and after 1945, are that although they were hard, not many people bothered with a door key because their front door was nearly always unlocked. Although by today's standards people could be considered to be generally poor and the social divide between the 'haves' and 'have-nots' was particularly great, trust led the way in just about every social relationship. To obtain a sense of the time it's worth remembering that toilets, for all but the wealthy few, were mostly outside affairs. For the users comfort, cut up newspapers could be found hanging on a reworked wire coat hanger attached to the back of the door. Coal fires were the normal heating source for almost every house and with no bathroom, a galvanised tub on the kitchen floor, topped up with kettles of boiling water, would be the order of the day. Clothes were mostly hand washed and hung on a line in the back yard, often catching the soot from smoky chimneys, or hung on a ceiling drying rack in the back room; a complicated device operated by a rope and pulley. Life was certainly much different then to the rather pampered and complex existence we suffer today, but social engagement at all levels was very high and in general society seemed to be much calmer. School discipline however was strict and if a child was not withdrawn from school by a desperate family to go to work, not many left it at the age of fifteen without having mastered the three 'R's'. Many individuals only owned one pair of shoes; a pair that would normally have to last a whole year, and a suit for young men in the 50s would often be a hand-me-down from father, brother or a close relative. Between the wars, living standards and social interaction for the average person were very similar except 'class' differences were much more pronounced. The centre of social activity and the main hub of problem solving for the working man would be 'The Pub' ... and there were nearly one hundred thousand of them in England and Wales during 1905 compared to less than forty eight thousand today (2015).

So, in a world of no National Health Service and the words 'politically correct' not yet even linked together, let alone used in everyday language, Tony was growing up. A common name for someone with a dark skin was obviously 'darkie' and often reference would be made to the term 'Golliwog' or shortened simply to 'Wog'. Enid Blyton had a golliwog character in her children's books until the

1980s; James Robertson and Sons, a famous jam manufacturer of the time, had a golliwog logo proudly adorning its product jars for many years and of course there was always the very popular Black and White Minstrels TV performances to entertain us on a Sunday afternoon. To confirm there was absolutely no 'political correctness' operating in the UK between the wars and for many years afterward, Alf Garnett appeared on our TV screens in the 60s and 70s giving popularity to the terms 'coon' and 'sambo'.

Racism as such and the use of derogatory names for people with dark or black skin was practiced and flourished, without hindrance, until the new millennium and even when openly acting in a racist manner or using racist terms became a matter of legality, the unfortunate mindset still existed in many walks of life, and the business that was Football was one of them. So, a person singled out as a 'darkie' had little choice living in the UK during the 20th Century but to be either patronised or ostracised by the white majority, and no one really seemed to care.

Tony Collins was, however, blessed with a strong character, possessing unusually resilient reserves of both mental and physical strength, allowing him to be the kind of man who would forge a pathway to success in a world of open prejudice. Furthermore, he chose to pursue a particularly prominent sporting occupation and one that was strictly limited to those who could maintain a disciplined regime of physical fitness combined with an exceptional ability on the field of play. This man's world was that of professional English football and one within which barriers were broken down and negative comment discarded by someone with determination to make it to the top … not only as a player, but as a team manager as well. Perhaps, as many informed observers thought at the time, Tony Collins, a young man with sparkling footwork and exceptional speed on the wing was one of the best football players that the England team never had. Surely though, the level of achievement he pushed himself toward as a player and manager would be enough for most, but for Tony Collins, it was just the beginning. He became the Guru of the science behind success in a sport which had relied very much upon brute force and ignorance to be a winning team. He was proclaimed to be 'The Teacher' by the National press and the 'Master Spy' by other English League team managers. At his peak, in the 70s, he was the backroom boy that everyone wanted, including the England manager of the day, Don Revie. When other managers and coaches were figuring out how to make their full-backs a stone heavier, six inches taller and ten percent angrier, Tony Collins was working out the tactical advantages of different forms of balanced play such as 4-4-1-1 and the original 4-4-2 set play positioning that has today become a standard in English football.

Tony Collins was the first black fully contracted manager in the English professional football league and still, in 2015, one of the very few ever to have arrived there. Many current internet links and articles of the time herald Keith Alexander as the first black professional English Football league manager, taking up his initial spell in that position with Lincoln City in 1993. However, this is untrue and after Collins, he was credited with actually being the second black manager in the League, a gap of some 30 plus years.

The question then has to be asked … 'what happened in between?' Well, as manager, Collins turned Rochdale A.F.C into a Fourth Division cup challenging team on a shoestring budget. He took Leeds United into Europe in no mean fashion under Don Revie, and Bristol City into the top flight division of the game as assistant manager in partnership with Alan Dicks.

Are there many stories to be told along the way? Of course there are. Kings of the game like Alex Ferguson, Brian Clough (his devastating 44 days in charge at Leeds United), Bill Shankley and Don Revie, along with players such as Kevin Keegan, Gordon McQueen and Norman Hunter all crossed the path of Tony Collins, with some better off for the experience than others. The doors to the boardrooms of English football are also prised open with interesting things to say about individuals such as Freddie Ratcliffe, Robert Hobbs and Manny Cussins. These are reflections and recollections that have never been revealed before due to Tony's reluctance to be interviewed by the media on matters that he felt should kept inside the sport and therefore not for public consumption.

The English game of professional football is today followed by millions and commands fees for broadcasting rights of over £5 billion (sterling). It consists of 72 teams in three divisions and a further associated league named the 'Football Conference' making up the English Football League System. Top flight players are now International super stars earning many millions a year in salaries, bonuses and product sponsorship, so in comparison, it is perhaps challenging to imagine the world into which Tony Collins was born; a world gripped between devastating wars, a country weighed down by inept politics along with its bigoted colonial past … and football players earning such a pittance wage they were forced to take off-season jobs to simply put food on the table. This was at a time when women still did not have an equal vote, and members of Parliament had only just been awarded an annual salary. Up until that point in 1911 only landed gentry or self-serving industrialists could afford to become an MP with the House of Commons being more of an exclusive boys club than a true house of legislature.

The United Kingdom was going through a massive period of change as a result of a poorly conceived and ill managed document known as 'the Armistice' which was supposed to have brought the Great War to an end. However, it would in effect end up simply being the spark that would survive long enough in the German psyche to start another, more devastating conflict in the years to come.

The Tough Twenties: The General Strike of May in the year Anthony Collins was born was soon to be seen as the tip of an iceberg in terms of what was to develop into the encroaching world economic collapse of the 1930s. Britain's world trade would fall by half; the country's registered unemployed would reach more than 3.0 million out of a total workforce of 17.0 million and many millions more would have to be satisfied with part time work only. The debt accumulated by most European countries to fund the Great War would cause a collapse in financial confidence that would have an unwanted effect throughout heavy industry, resulting in manpower reductions unsustainable by the fledgling British welfare system known commonly as 'the dole'. As a result, tensions would run high amongst the working population and simmering prejudice at all levels of society would come violently to the fore.

Anthony Norman (Tony) Collins arrived into this world of economic, political and social uncertainty on March 19th, 1926 in North Kensington, London, England to the delight of Lou Collins … his white British mother. Tony Collins was dark skinned and for his seventeen year old, unmarried parent … there would be consequences!

PART ONE

A Life in Black and White

CHAPTER ONE

An Unceremonious Arrival

The events leading up to the birth of the Collins child, who would be known to his family and all around him simply as 'Tony', was surrounded in some level of mystery. A young, frightened but determined Lou Collins refused to give up the name of the father or the level of association she had enjoyed with him, and when Tony finally took his first breath in the stark, near militarily managed surroundings of the Kensington Hospital Maternity Unit, everyone understood why. In 1926, the most cardinal of sins was to give birth to a child out of wedlock and sitting closely alongside this heinous social crime would be the fathering of a mixed race child. It was obvious to all around this attractive and kind natured teenage white girl on March 19th, 1926 that she had somehow 'fallen by the wayside' and the attending doctors, midwives and nurses did little to hide their feelings on the matter.

The obvious question was asked many times in relation to the identity of the father but Lou Collins remained tight lipped. She would later bear children with an African partner known to be someone named Bennie Ghanje, or possibly Mayange. Whatever the family name spelling, most would address him simply as Bennie G. Lou would also make the rather brave choice to care for her mixed race children herself; resigned to bear the insults and stigma attached to such a situation. However, with the birth of Tony, she had to make a decision. There was obvious pressure from many sides to give up the child in a world where racist feelings were running high against blacks and coloureds although many British soldiers had fought side by side with Indian, African and Caribbean troops during the Great War. They had lived the same life as the white troops, suffered the same indignities associated with survival and acted just as bravely with over 4 million black soldiers fighting in the First World War and many thousands dying for Britain. One recalls that …

'They called us darkies, but when the battle starts, it didn't make a difference. We were all the same. When you're there, you don't care about anything. Every man there is under the rifle!'

After the controversy surrounding the arrival of her healthy baby boy, Lou refused point blank to give up her child to anyone but her parents, so Kit (Eliza Mary) and Wilfred Collins came into Tony's life and what a good, loving association and relationship it would turn out to be. Tony would refer for the rest of his life to Wilfred as his Dad and to Kit as his Mum with Lou being recognized by him as his Sister. The Collins family were working class people seen by many as good, kind and proud individuals who didn't have much and rented a two storey house at 397 Portobello Road. Rental today of a property in this now highly fashionable part of London would hit your pocket for several thousands of pounds sterling per month, but in 1926, the Portobello Road area was rather run down, supporting a lively working class community epitomizing the image of London life and was the centre of a still active and world renowned street market.

Lou gave up Tony to her parents with great reluctance but she knew that unless she did so, her life ahead and that of her child would be put to trial with literally nowhere to live, no husband and father to care for them, no job and every door of opportunity closed to a white woman with a black child. Black people were forced to live in their own communities consisting mainly of poor quality housing and left to find limited work in the docks; work that would be of a very menial nature. The true facts of the matter were that at such an unfortunate time in British history, she, as a white woman could not live in a black man's world, and a black man could naturally not live in hers. Even as late as 1944 Kit would write to Tony, who was at that time conscripted into the British Army, about the plight of Bennie G, the African partner of his birth mother, Lou.

> *'Bennie was unable to get work on account of his colour, he applied for a job and he was refused because of that. At the labour they told him that he was a problem and did not know what to do with him as he was black. I was refused to rent a flat here in London because the landlady objected to coloured people living in her house.'*

Further painful experiences suffered by Lou brought home the point quite forcibly and she writes again as follows.

> *'Another incident when I applied for a loan from the Public Assistance Offices in 1938, I was told by the receiving officer I should be ashamed to have a negro husband and black children, mum will tell you all about it when you see her because you were only a little boy then.'*

Over the years, Lou would never cease to be shocked and humiliated by the way she was treated by white British people, particularly in London, and it would leave her bitter and uncompromising throughout the rest of her life.

So, one way or another, the pathway was to be set for Anthony

Norman Collins. Dad Wilfred worked long, hard hours as an upholsterer for a coach company whilst Mum Kit was left to keep order in a house that was also occupied by Marge, Cyril, Stan, Jack and Berne, all of whom Tony would come to regard as his brothers and sisters. Surrounded by this close family unit, Tony enjoyed a happy childhood and was unashamedly spoilt with love and genuine affection. Stan and Jack regularly joked around and Cyril, being more private and shy, was someone who thought the world of Tony and would later in life closely follow his professional career.

Family holidays were taken quite regularly with Kit having a close friend who lived in the seaside town of Margate and when she went to visit, she would take Tony with her. The two of them also had days out at another seaside resort of Clacton on Sea, but Dad Wilfred never went with them and it wasn't until some years later that Tony discovered the reason why. There was simply not enough money to stretch to all three of them going together and once Tony became 16 years old, he vowed to himself that Kit and Wilfred would never need to spend another penny on him ever again … and they didn't!

~~~~

The life of Tony Collins therefore began at 397 Portobello Road and as far as he was concerned, Kit and Wilfred were firmly established as his parents; the people who would look after him, care for him, support him and provide him with a love of family that would follow him for the rest of his life. Portobello Road is a street in the Notting Hill district of the Royal Borough of Kensington and Chelsea located in West London. It runs the length of Notting Hill from north to south and on Saturdays hosts its own famous outdoor market. In 1926, the area was considered to be grubby and the often ill-maintained properties had not changed much since the latter part of the 19th Century. It was regarded unkindly by some as consisting mainly of 'slum' accommodation, but whatever anyone thought of the Portobello Road and its residents, to a young Tony Collins it was home.

School can be a cruel environment for an individual displaying any form of difference from the mainstream be it religion, ethnicity or disability. So when he attended Buckingham Terrace Junior School, he not only experienced his first encounter with academia but exposure to the early, often innocent questioning of his identity. However, Tony conquered just about all that was placed in front of him and his school report dated March 31st, 1936 contained the following remarks concerning his placement as number five in a class of forty four pupils.

'Tony has been working well and deserves his position in class which is composed of many older boys'

His progress was noted as 'Excellent', his attendance as 'Regular' and from marks received in all his tests, it appeared that one Anthony Collins was bright and doing well at school. At the age of 11 he moved to North Kensington Central School in St Marks Road, W.10 and in his school report for the term ending October, 1938, two things became obvious. The first was that he could be considered as nothing else other than athletically gifted and the other was he had grown to enjoy the sound of his own voice. His final position in class was 18 out of 42. His marks for Physical Education were 23 out of 25 and once again noted as 'Excellent'.

His class master would write … *'Settled down well at the beginning of the year showing that he has ability. He has lately become talkative!'*

5

Although he was more than capable of holding his own in most academic subjects, Tony's first love was sport and it would not be long before he began to excel in many sporting activities. His school master, a Mr. Davies, noticed how keen Tony was on the game of football and would each night give him a 'Casey' ball to take home and practice with. This was an expensive item during its day and consisted of a rubber bladder which could be pumped up hard and contained within a leather case made up of several stitched parts. The bladder opening was laced tight when the ball was fully pumped up. Each morning, without fail, Tony would return the football to Mr. Davies and perhaps this kind act by a caring teacher, would be the one to set Tony on the path to success as a professional football player, finding his place amongst some of the greatest exponents of the game and playing for some of the most respected clubs within the English Football League.

Tony's love of sport carried him through to proudly represent his school in the Kensington Schools Athletics Competition and he was down to take part in nearly every event, although he did actually give his place away in the high jump category to a friend of his so they could both go to the event together. As a result of his taking part that day, he became the Long Jump Champion, bringing home his first medal for the Kensington Schools Sports Association.

During this very formative period of his life, Tony took up the role of captain of the school football team and he managed to hold the whole team together without needing to address any racial issues. At such a young age, this was a remarkable achievement and was credited to his very strong and skilful physical ability combined with a resilient personality and great humour. Tony Collins was a likeable and popular character who was not only a strong competitor but showed his considerable people management skills at an age when most of his contemporaries would be struggling to contend with the inevitable complexities of their early teenage years. Tony was focused on people and sport and knew even then that there was a route somewhere that would allow him to continue his love of both when his educational years were over. His final school days were spent at the Bovington Road Emergency School in Golborne Road where his popularity was confirmed with the voting of pupils and staff alike to confirm his position as School Captain. In 1940, his headmaster Mr. Mitchell would write in a letter of reference …

'His educational attainments are well up to the average. He was chosen by the pupils to be Captain of the School which is testimony to their opinion of him and their choice was endorsed by the school staff. He is an excellent sportsman and I would have no hesitation in strongly recommending this boy.'

However, not all was easy going at that period in Tony's life and on some occasions his social situation and background could not be ignored. For example, he went for a trial to play cricket for the London area but was put off when he arrived at the ground in his grey school trousers and all the other boys were in cricket whites. He was perhaps unnecessarily embarrassed because his school trousers were all he had, but that experience put him off playing cricket for life, holding firmly to the opinion that this was a game for boys from a more affluent background … and that is a view he continued to maintain for many years. Tony also held a similar opinion about tennis, feeling that again, this was more a sport for 'those with' rather than 'those without'!

He was not only blessed with a swift pair of feet and sharp mind, Tony also possessed a good singing voice and was quickly taken up by St. Augustine's Church for their choir. This gave him his first opportunity to ride in a car as part of the choir detailed to sing Christmas carols to some of the larger and more affluent properties surrounding the Kensington district. Tony saw this as a great prospect to catch a glimpse of 'how the other half lived' and to earn some extra pocket money.

~~~~

As the Collins boy carried on forging a reputation at school for his considerable athletic skills, the dark clouds of war were once again gathering over Europe. The Armistice agreement that stopped hostilities in 1918 had fuelled the rise of Herr Hitler looking for some reparations with a vengeance and so at 11:15 on September 3rd, 1939 the British Prime Minister, Neville Chamberlain, announced to a disappointed nation that Britain was at war once again with Germany.

For a 13 year old boy from the Portobello Road, life would change dramatically. Beginning on September 7th, 1940 London was carpet bombed for 57 consecutive nights. Tony and his family would take shelter in the underground railway Tube stations and on some days he and his classmates would be allowed to leave school early, giving them time to get home before the sirens rang out their dismal warning sign that German bombers would be overhead shortly. The family would take 'Bob' their old dog with them to the shelters and meet with many familiar faces as they all huddled down together listening to the continuous boom of high explosive raining down on the streets above them.

It was a particularly horrific experience for a young boy barely in his teens and would make an impression that would stay with him for a very long time. When everyone left the shelter each morning after the 'all clear', it would be daylight and through the thick, choking fumes of toxic smoke fuelled by row upon row of burning buildings and some active Phosphorus incendiary bombs, often still laying in the street, Tony would rush to his part of the Portobello Road to see if his house was still there.

Plans for the evacuation of children from large cities were put into effect as the 'Blitz' continued on relentlessly. Many hundreds of thousands of children were moved out of London as part of these plans, all of which were issued with a small case for clothing, a haversack, gas masks and a label tied to their coats indicating which school they had come from, along with their name. There was no doubt it was all a most stressful process as children were assembled at their schools and led through the gates with their teachers to the railway stations. Mothers lined the streets as their children passed by holding each other's hands tightly. They would shout messages through their tears such as 'Don't forget to write!' and 'Make sure you wash behind your ears!' It was a highly charged emotional situation and would have a lasting effect on everyone concerned, especially the children.

Tony did not want to go, but his dad thought it best and that was how he came to be billeted at a large house in Medmenham near Henley on Thames. His school master quickly discovered the extent of Tony's sporting history. Not wishing to waste any time and with some obvious enthusiasm, he quickly formed and began to organise, a football team. Tony was made captain and led a group of boys that could easily beat the best the local town could offer and to make it more interesting the smitten teacher offered a prize of 'tuppence' (two old pennies) for every goal scored. So, that was Tony Collins' sweet money sorted … and with this fairly guaranteed new source of income, he would be in charge of buying all the sweets and handing them out to his pals.

However, for a homesick Tony, apart from the football, he really did not want to stay in the country, so when his mum and dad visited one day, he persuaded them to take him back home to London with them. He had experienced enough of the countryside and wanted to be where he felt he belonged – in London with the people who were precious to him. His premise was that if they were to finally succumb to a German bomb, then he would want to be with them. There was resistance from his family of course. But his reasoning was simple and direct … and it worked!

CHAPTER TWO

Your Country Needs You

The war years for Tony were ones of simple survival through to the age of 17 and football continued to be a large and increasing part of his busy social life. He followed the game at both Queens Park Rangers and West Ham football clubs although no league fixtures were played during the war years. He began to regularly attend the sports club at Acton United, just about 40 minutes away from home by bus and fortunately for Tony, Brentford Football Club also used the same training ground. They had an arrangement with Acton to 'spot' any promising youngsters and so it came about that Tony was picked to play for Acton United and shortly afterward signed as a junior player with the Brentford Bees.

It was an exciting time of life for Tony Collins. He had been signed by a football club, had managed to secure an apprenticeship with a local tool-making firm after leaving school and everything in his life appeared to be moving in the right direction. However, in 1944, although the tides of war had turned significantly in favour of Britain and its allies, to the point of serious planning for an invasion of Europe, the dreaded word 'conscription' was on the lips of every young boy about to turn 18 years of age.

So it was that on January 4th, 1944 he received the unwelcome letter advising him he was to attend a medical and the relevant preliminaries to serving his National Military Service. This process was all to take place at the Holy Trinity Church Hall in nearby Hounslow. It wasn't a shock of course; he knew it was coming and being a perfectly fit specimen, he was finally ordered to attend the General Service Corps, Number 52 Primary Training Wing at Britannia Barracks in Norwich, Norfolk. The fateful date was Thursday, April 6th, 1944 and with the letter of instruction, noted as reference SHP 34193, came a travel warrant and a payment of four shillings in respect of advance service pay. With the loyalty payment commonly known as the 'King's shilling' now reluctantly accepted, Tony Collins would shortly be on his way to war!

His dad, Wilfred was quite openly devastated that his youngest boy had been called to fight and both Kit and Lou Collins were determined to make some sort of effort to have the order rescinded. Tony however, was willing and happy to go. He had no desire to be, or seen to be different to any of his peers, but Lou was distraught, feeling that she and her family had been persecuted enough over the years for carrying the burden of nurturing black children and having a black husband. With some determination, she set out to bring the law onto her side.

~~~~

Born in Abeokuta, Nigeria, Oladipo Felix Solanke was a lawyer and political activist who campaigned on West African issues and was responsible for the setting up of a hostel for displaced West African individuals in London known as Africa House. In 1925, he founded the West African Students Union (WASU) with Herbert Bankole-Bright and became Secretary-General to the organisation.

Lou and Kit made approaches to Solanke to make a case in relation to the reduction of service for Tony from military to civilian. Within the first few days of his arrival at Norwich, several letters arrived from Lou and Kit advising him of some documentation that would require Tony's signature before it could be submitted to the courts … and on April 12th, Lou wrote the following.

'I was so pleased to hear from you and to know that so far you are OK You will have heard from mum by now that we both went to see Mr Solanke yesterday and he is going to take your case up for you. I explained to him how I (your mother) had been treated by the British people in this country because of Bennie being coloured also your brothers and sisters.'

On the 18th of April Lou also wrote …

'Well Tony, I went to Mr Solanke last Friday evening and he will be sending you some papers to sign about this weekend. Just do what he suggests and I feel everything will come alright for you. You can guess I am going to fight hard for you because your dad and I have been so badly treated in this country, not only your dad and I but when you were all small, I used to have as you know a very hard job even to get a place to live because of your colour. As I have said so many times, if your dad (Bennie) is not good enough for a decent job in this country then you my son, are not good enough to fight. Mr Solanke is sending all your dad's letters where they refused (in writing) to give him a job because of his colour.'

She added …

'I don't see any difference in going to jail and being in the army … your own body is not your own. I would like to know where this thing called 'Freedom' comes in!'

Lou's basic point was hammered home with regularity and for Tony, Norfolk seemed to be a very long way away from the London he loved and the people who truly loved him. It should be noted that although Tony called his grandparents (Kit and Wilfred) mum and dad, his birth mother Lou Collins often described herself in her letters to Tony as 'mum' and her partner Bennie G as 'dad'.

There would be little family love in the army and this was made abundantly clear to him when he reported to Norfolk and was given an unmeasured uniform known as a 'guess' size. He was assigned to the REME (Royal Electrical & Mechanical Engineers) and after being issued with their uniforms of sorts, the group that included Tony attended their first instructional meeting.

Everyone appeared in surprisingly good spirits as many were laughing, joking and stealing a quick smoke. However, this came to an abrupt end when an officer advised they would all be going to Burma and if captured by the enemy, not to resist or else they would "get the bayonet!". The next morning, nearly half the conscripts were missing from parade.

~~~~

Eventually, with basic training completed and supposedly knowing one end of a rifle from another, a not quite so eager 18 year old A. Collins was sent off to face the enemy. His battalion were loaded on a ship heading east and when his troop were called to 'muster' in order to rehearse emergency evacuation procedures, they donned lifejackets with little enthusiasm and a certain level of trepidation cloaked by typically brave conscript wisecracks. However, when making passage through the English Channel, the very first attack warning siren sounded accompanied by the vibrating, muted 'crump' of depth charges exploding very near to them. The escorting gunships were doing their job and it was possibly at that very point the severity and seriousness of the dangerous adventure they were all embarked upon came sharply home.

However, luck was on their side as once established sailing so far unharmed through the Bay of Biscay, the fresh faced young and inexperienced troops were told the good news. They were being diverted … for whatever reason, and once docked in the Bay of Naples, a lucky CFN (Private) 14735335 A. Collins discovered he was to stay there, with all disturbing thoughts of a possibly hot and sticky end in some god forsaken Burmese jungle fading fast.

Welcome to 693 Base Manufacturing Workshops, REME, Naples!

Now, real army life would begin for Tony Collins. He was quickly recognised as being physically fit and with military logic coming to the fore, was given the uncertain task of getting the other troops stationed with him 'into shape'. With his good humour and no rank to hide behind, he took up his responsibilities with enthusiasm, drilling and sweating his comrades to a level of physical fitness that many had not enjoyed before.

His working role was as a mechanic and driver to senior officers, a job he took to easily being a generally good people person. Obviously his colour was an evident distinction and as will happen, anywhere in the world, wherever a group of young men collect, a nickname would become an essential first part of the formation of any enduring comradeship. If you were from Scotland, you were called 'Jock'. If you were from Newcastle you would likely be named 'Geordie' and if your family name was white, you would no doubt be re-titled 'Chalky'. Tony would not be excluded from such a club and therefore the inevitable name of 'Darkie Boy' would follow him throughout his contented but not outstanding military career.

However, everyone who knew Tony also knew he was not someone to be messed with. At five feet nine inches tall and weighing in at a steady 135 pounds, he took up boxing which he didn't particularly like but being quick on his feet, having good balance and lightning reactions, he was naturally good at it.

Some of the unfortunate youngsters who were conscripted at that time came from a background that had included periods of incarceration in some very strict young offender institutions known as Borstals. These boys were often tough, uncompromising, anti-social and ready to become physical at the slightest provocation. Such a young man was included in Tony's platoon and one day 'it all kicked off'. The platoon senior PT Officer quickly intervened telling the other lads to form a circle so that an ordered boxing match could begin. Needless to say, Tony with his doubtless finely tuned boxing skills won a popular victory and after that the Borstal Boy gave Darkie Boy much more respect.

In effect, the war for Tony Collins was turning out much better than expected. He had what many would see as a 'cushy' posting in Italy and 639 Platoon formed a football team, playing other units in the area. As is the British way, once a game of football is established, a league will follow very shortly … and a physical trophy of some description soon after that. Tony became the heart of the team and as such 639 Platoon won the league and the cup trophy on regular occasions. After the war, Tony's pal Tom would write to his mother a few quite moving words as follows.

Dear Mrs Collins

Tony has been a fellow inmate of the grand and famous club namely the

Army. Frankly my year with your son has been the most eventful and happy year I have had the pleasure to remember, we were more than just mates, although at times we had our little differences which I think was due to the surroundings. We at 693 had the pleasure in watching him play football and I'm looking forward to seeing him play in the near future as a professional. Tony played a very prominent part in 693's many victories. This was of course the general talk of 693, a grand lad and a great footballer.'

During this period of popularity amongst his pals and peers, Tony managed to create a less than politically correct situation when he organised a challenge match with some of the locally held German POWs. His commanding officer was less than pleased, pointing out to Tony there would be some very unwelcome consequences for the British if the POWs won the game. It was something to do with "stiff upper lips" and "reputation of the regiment old chap" along with the type of conversation that could simply not be had over cocktails in a world Tony Collins quite obviously did not live in. However, good fortune and not a small amount of skill ensured that Tony scored several goals in the game, beating the Germans fair and square leaving him under no illusions that such a mistake was not to be made again.

Day to day life in the army and living in Italy could perhaps have been seen by Tony as a bit of an adventure. He and his fellow soldiers lived in small single storey bungalow style houses that were best described as basic but comfortable and only a few minutes' walk from the cook house. The camp had acquired a dog that used to run around the area when the football team were training and naturally, many attempted to 'shoo' it away in case it became a hindrance. However, one day, the commanding general visited and told the men to leave the dog alone and from that moment on, Tony thought the general to be a be a 'grand chap'!

As a driver mechanic, Tony's day to day work was very varied and when not driving officers around Italy he would be detailed to travel into Naples town to collect rations etc. Once the vehicle stopped of course, out of nowhere would appear the local children, the 'urchins' of Naples who were only just surviving in the depths of poverty. It was often a distressing sight to be surrounded by bare footed ragged individuals, some no older than four or five, running up to the car or truck shouting '*Corporale … corporale, cigarette, chocolate, bisquitte por poppa!*' Everyone the children met was of course a corporal and although they shouted for food or something to be taken back to their 'Poppa', unfortunately, not many actually had one.

Tony used to carry out a regular stores and rations run that ended at the officers mess and there was always one little boy waiting patiently for him and his accompanying Italian minders. The minders were a necessary evil to ensure the wheels and any other removable items would still be attached to his vehicle if he ever left it to attend to paperwork or collect goods in Naples town. This child was six or seven years old and suffered from obvious malnutrition. Tony would fill his bag with any surplus tinned food for the boy who would offer a salute and a '*grazi corporale*' before running off with his trophies.

Drivers were often called upon to move vehicles to northern Italy, Austria and sometimes Germany, coming back to barracks by train and stopping on the way at 'feed halts' to pick up haversack rations for the journey. The children of course mobbed the railway stations everywhere they went and when any excess or uneaten rations were available, they would give it away to the kids. Whereas the Italian children would run away immediately, the German children were far more disciplined and cautious. At one such stop, Tony called a thin, underweight looking German child over who seemed almost embarrassed at having to beg for his survival and after expressing his obvious thanks to the English soldier for his gifts of food, he turned to leave, but after a pause, he again turned back and pulled a little enamel badge from inside his ragged coat. He gave it wordlessly to Tony as a sign of his thanks and to confirm that what had just taken place between them was not necessarily a gift, but a transaction … a trade of sorts. This small badge was truly his only precious possession and the episode moved everyone who witnessed it to tears, especially private Tony Collins who would keep it as one of *his* most precious possessions … for the rest of his life! He learnt later that German children would share out any food they obtained equally with others whereas this was not necessarily the case with the 'urchins' of Naples!

When not driving, soldiers with a trade would work and were given jobs to fit their particular skills. Tony was allocated duties as a lathe operator; a job he enjoyed and in managing his time carefully, along with others, he could arrange to have windows of time off to enjoy the local sights and entertaining offerings of the local 'tavernas'. The atmosphere at that time was generally good and British troops would be treated well by the local population. However, one particular spot, a short road tunnel, was well known by servicemen as a place to avoid knowing that some disgruntled locals would often throw fireworks at the military vehicles passing through … which were to them the irritating emblem of occupation. The Italian Mafia were in regular and obvious view and could often be seen in their fast power boats running contraband across the bay of Naples. This again annoyed the locals and Italian authorities alike. Sometimes the police would give chase, but mostly the response was one of apathy with many of them directly involved with the Mafia families and therefore reluctant to take any action.

~~~~

Tony's football career could probably be said to have started then, in the army. The local football club Padova saw him play and wanted to sign him when he was released from military service, but not being able to speak Italian, he decided it was possibly not the right move for him. So, a young, impressionable and fairly unworldly 18 year old boy had entered his majesties armed forces in 1944 and was to be repatriated back to UK and honourably released from service in 1947 as a bright, physically fit and street-wise 21 year old man. There was no doubting the fact that Tony had learnt a lot in the army; a lot about life in general, the use and misuse of authority and the establishment of bonds of real friendship. He learnt how to be a team player and how to lead from the front … when necessary. He had of course acquired other skills such as how to drive a vehicle and how to repair it, but the country he was going back to had changed substantially in the aftermath of war and to many returning soldiers, it would not necessarily be remembered as the one they had left …!

CHAPTER THREE

Search for a New Beginning

So, for Anthony Norman Collins, his life and time in the British Army brought with it many advantages and kick started substantial changes in his life, some of which were immediately obvious, especially whilst he was in Italy … and others not so. The obvious were his new found skills and opportunity to travel, along with the experiences that such a prospect provided. He was able to witness, first hand, the depravations of war along with acts of crass brutality alongside often unexpected and spontaneous acts of unbelievable kindness and selflessness. The 'not so obvious' were the contacts he had made in Italy; contacts that would shape his life forever in terms of meeting a wife and entering his very first contract as a professional football player.

The day that a very attractive and confident Edith Murdoch came into Tony's life was unremarkable in that this young Sheffield lass was having an adventure of her own in the magnificent Palace at Caserta. She was the confidential secretary to the Director of Mechanical Engineering (REME) and they caught one another's eye on Tony's visits to the Palace, but that was about all. They never spoke as far as he can remember and as he didn't attend any of the dances regularly organised by the NAAFI (Navy, Army and Air Force Institute) which was the recognised meeting place for young men and young women in the forces, he denied himself the chance to make further contact with Edith. Looking back, perhaps the reason he avoided such high profile social events was that he may have been somewhat self conscious about his colour. Young, attractive girls were in short supply in Italy, as they were elsewhere in a decimated post-war Europe and British soldiers normally came second in choice to 'the Yanks' (American soldiers) who were paid more and had access to sought-after gifts such as cigarettes, chocolate and certain rare items of female clothing.

Therefore the army and the time he spent serving its cause in Italy, was the place he would first meet his future wife … although he was not to know it at the time. It would also be the cause for a certain Private Ibbotson to write to the manager of an English second division football team to tell him how impressed he was with the talents of a particular Mr Collins. On April 9th, 1946, the manager of Sheffield Wednesday, Eric Taylor, would write to Tony …

'I have had you recommended by Pte. Ibbotson of C.M.F., as a promising inside left, and I extend to you an invitation to take part in a trial with us at the earliest date convenient to yourself. I look forward to having an early reply from you, and enclose stamped addressed envelope.'

This letter would trigger two events. The first would be the start of his career as a footballer, but the second would be the meeting once again of his future wife!

Edith Murdoch was born on November 7th, 1923. She was from Sheffield, a northern English city in Yorkshire, the heartland of the British steel industry. During the war, Edith's sisters took up work in the armament factories of Sheffield and the surrounding areas, but Edith had ambitions to do more with her life and signed on with the

Army in 1942 as a shorthand typist trained in secretarial duties. She was considered by those around her to be somewhat ambitious, open minded, self assured and purposeful, eventually taking up what was regarded as the 'plumb' secretarial position at the Caserta Palace before moving on to the REME General Headquarters where Tony was stationed. She loved Italy along with the camaraderie and the particular lifestyle that being part of the military forces offered her. She noted that until she joined the Army, she didn't even own her own toothbrush and the possibility of returning to Sheffield would only be regarded by her as something of an anti-climax.

However, fate played its hand expertly in that unless an impressed Mr Ibbotson had not written to Eric Taylor and Eric not offered Tony a trial, Tony Collins would never have had cause or reason to travel to Sheffield and naturally, would never have met Edith again. So, where did they actually first make contact after the war?

Was it perhaps like something out of the movies?

Well, in fact it was just such an event as when Tony was out at a cinema in Sheffield one evening, he was saying goodbye to his friends, turned and there she was … standing right in front of him. They recognised one another straight away from their time in Italy and started talking. The rest, as they say, is history!

Edith recalls that Tony was a 'shy fellow' when it came to courting. When he moved up to Sheffield after being demobbed from the military and signed by Sheffield Wednesday, he found himself living with a Mr and Mrs Jimmy Rowley at 69 Hawksley Road, Hillsborough and fortunately quite near the Wednesday main ground. To get to the training ground however, Tony had to pass Edith's house on the Halifax road each day and with a bit of a push and shove from Edith, their relationship blossomed. He was gifted with the type of personality that all mothers loved, which was fortunate for both of them as a white woman courting a 'coloured' man in the 1940s would attract a certain level of attention … much of it unwanted and nearly all of it unflattering. However, Edith's mother thought Tony was a 'lovely chap' and so, with her blessing and possible encouragement, the romance took hold.

In the February of 1948, valentine's cards were exchanged between Edith and Tony and they married on August 6th 1949, spending their honeymoon in a small caravan on the Yorkshire coast near Filey; a little luxury owned by Edith's older sister Lily.

~~~~

Tony's life was football. He thought of little else and perhaps the reason he was able to consider marriage and a long term commitment to Edith was down more to her determination and resourcefulness than his. But Edith was good for Tony, there was no doubting that. She was a couple of years older than him and many would consider perhaps she provided the necessary emotional security and support that would allow him to pursue his career as a football player and then as a manager … without distraction!

It all started with the Ibbotson letter to the manager of Sheffield Wednesday, Eric Taylor. Eric was a man dedicated to his trade and would often end a telephone conversation with "Keep as cheerful as you can …" a philosophy that exemplified a man who was essentially an extrovert showman. Eric was not a footballer and had never played the game. He was an administrator, a manipulator of people and an outstanding club manager. However, like managers of all other English clubs, the war had decimated its ranks and the professional football leagues would need to be rebuilt … from the training pitch up!

After the end of the Second World War, all was not rosy in Britain and the scourge of food rationing was not due to finally end for some years to come. The Football League was suspended in 1939 and reformed in 1946 with a First Division, Second Division, Third Division (North) and Third Division (South). Sheffield Wednesday, named 'the Owls' by its fans, started the post war league years in the second division and it was going to be a fight to get promoted out of it. Every manager, in every league was looking for the same thing in 1946 … the best, most talented football players in the country. So when Eric Taylor made a connection with Tony, he had no intention of letting it drop. After making initial contact with the young soldier in April 1946, Eric pursued it further with a letter on the 10th of May. He then renewed contact in January 1947 and on 29th April offering to play Tony when he arrived in UK on leave. During the May of 1947, Tony played several times for the Wednesday in the Central League and his trial was noted by an unidentified reporter and similarly unidentified newspaper clipping of the day as follows.

'One Trial Enough – Several southern clubs are watching the grand Central League displays by Sheffield Wednesday's inside-left, Albert Collins.'

The article went on to explain the contents of the Ibbotson letter to Eric Taylor and Eric's subsequent contact with Tony Collins. It described Tony's trip to Hillsborough and highlighted the fact that London clubs had simply allowed a good, local player to escape them. It is worth noting that Tony was misreported and had suddenly become 'Albert' for some unknown reason, with this incorrect name unfortunately sticking for a short while. On August 11th, 1947, Eric Taylor wrote to Tony commenting upon the good news regarding his demobilisation from the forces, telling him he would be 'very pleased' to see him on his return. So it came about that in 1947, true to his word, Eric Tayor signed Tony Collins as a professional football player for Sheffield Wednesday. After they signed the papers, they both checked the train timetables to get Tony back to London and Eric took the opportunity to slip something into his pocket. When he was on the train, Tony felt in his pocket to find a ten pound note … his signing-on fee! Tony felt at that moment as if he had 'won the pools' and become an overnight millionaire, with 10 pounds sterling in 1947 equating to around 450 pounds sterling of buying power at today's rates. His contracted wages were £7.0.0 a week in the playing season and £5.0.0 a week in the closed season, equivalent to around £308.00 and £220.00 in today's money. As a point of interest, Tony confirms the first team players were earning around £12.0.0 a week on contract, equivalent to over £500.00 a week by comparison.

So, Tony Collins was definitely on his way up; signed with a good club in the second division and although only playing with the reserves, the platform of regular play would provide him with an opportunity to show what he could do … and that was all he asked for! The local newspapers had found a new star to follow with comments from anonymous sports reporters such as:

Against Yorkshire Amateurs: '… *combined well with Collins who finished off a great effort with a capital goal'*
Against South Kirby: *'Collins scored for Wednesday from a penalty'*
Against Gainsborough: *'The Owls were constantly aggressive, Collins was particularly prominent'*
Against Blackpool Reserves: '… *and Woodhead and Collins, the best wing on the field got one each'*
Against Sheffield United A: '*and Collins equalised with a brilliant shot'*
Against West Bromwich Albion Reserves: '… *brought an equaliser, Collins turning a centre from Woodhead into the net'*

The accolades would continue. Tony Collins had what it took to be a first class professional football player, but after a war that had scarred the memories of many and with few real jobs to come back to in a country that had been driven to the brink of bankruptcy, literally everyone else with a modicum of talent wanted to become a professional sportsman ... and the competition was necessarily fierce. Tony had one other attribute that made him stand out from many others ... he was recognisably one of the few black players in the game of professional football and prejudices were often ill-concealed.

If the question had ever been asked as to why such a good, talented and most importantly 'goal scoring' player could not break into the first team squad at Sheffield Wednesday, you would probably be told by a reflective Tony Collins it was due to the high number of International players already contracted there. However, he would also be able to recall the fact that the trainer, whose name has disappeared into another, distant memory, would always give Tony a pair of boots that were too small for him. They used to cripple his feet and he had to spend many hours sitting in the bath with them on in an attempt to stretch them. When he complained he would be told by the callous trainer that wearing tight boots would 'toughen him up!' His feet would therefore remain sore throughout his time with Wednesday and he would regularly lose toenails after that. However, complaints and not attending training, in such a competitive environment, would mean being dropped from the team. This may have been part of someone's plan on the training staff ... but it certainly was not part of Tony's!

He maintained a good relationship with Eric Taylor, looking up to him as a manager and as a human being. He was a man driven by the sport he was so proud of, and everyone in the game respected him. However, no matter how good Tony's relationship with his manager was and no matter how many goals he scored for the reserves and the

'A' team, two seasons down from his signing day, he would see little chance of playing in the first team. This was a disappointment, but not a setback, and with a new wife to provide for and a family to start, Tony Collins knew he would have to consider a move. Despite not seeing any progress into the higher levels of the game, the local sports journalists loved him, keeping his name at the forefront of their match reports with comments such as those below taken from unnamed sports reporters in unidentified newspaper cuttings of the time.

"Owls' Disputed Goal Makes Villa Howl"

'Wakeman pushed upwards a red-hot drive from Collins … the referee, who was right on the spot had no hesitation in awarding a goal!'

"Quick Reverse for City Reserves"

'… Marriott won a corner for Wednesday from which Collins scored'

"Ossett v Wednesday"

'… Wednesday took the lead through Collins from a penalty'

"Wednesday v Everton"

'Success came in six minutes, when Collins deceived Burnett with a low shot which passed just inside the post'

"Coopers Struggle With Sheffield"

'It was no surprise when Collins equalised'

Although Tony Collins was not the first black or coloured player in the English football league, he wasn't far behind. The earliest recorded players are Arthur Wharton, of mixed parentage and shortly after, Walter Tull. Many football fans today firmly believe that the sixties or maybe the fifties saw the first black players in the League … but this is far from true. Wharton was signed by Rotherham United in 1889 playing as goal-keeper and after five years he moved on to Sheffield United. Walter Tull was an outfield player of West Indian descent who originally played for Tottenham until 1910 and then signed for Northampton Town, making 110 appearances for the club between 1911 and 1914. To mark Walter Tull's achievements, not only as a footballer but also as an officer in the British Army throughout the First World War, a memorial was opened at Northampton Town in 1999. A significant part of the text described on the memorial stone reads:

'Through his actions WDJ Tull ridiculed the barriers of ignorance that tried to deny people of colour equality with their contemporaries'

Between the war years, there were a small number of black players signed with a variety of clubs and as evidenced from the great research work carried out by historian Phil Vasili, it is quite obvious that most, if not all of these players were subject to obvious discrimination and racial prejudice in the dressing room, on the pitch and in their social life. Once the league started again in 1946, the reset button had to be pressed and black players were not prominent in many club signings, making Tony Collins if not the first, then one of the very earliest black players to appear in the league after the war closely followed by names such as Lloyd 'Lindy' Delapenha, Charlie Williams and a little later Giles Heron. R.H. Brown, who was signed as an apprentice for Stoke City in 1938, resumed his contract when the league started again in 1946.

As 1949 approached, Tony felt there was little chance of any further progress with Sheffield Wednesday and with his new responsibilities, a burning ambition and the hunger to simply play football with what he considered to be the very best players in the world, in front of a crowd … he knew he would have to make a move from Sheffield

Wednesday. Although there is no official record available to confirm the number of goals scored by Tony Collins for Sheffield Wednesday playing in the club's second team, the total was significant and newspaper cuttings of the day can confirm more than a dozen.

Eric Taylor the 'Owls' manager, although perhaps a little short on emotion, was considered an approachable kind of person by most who worked with him and more significantly, the players who played for him. He had risen to the heights of Manager from a lowly beginning as an office boy and had the name of 'Wednesday' engraved on his soul. He was asked to take over as Secretary-Manager in 1942, on a temporary basis, which turned into a permanent position, held without interruption for 16 years. Tony held a great deal of respect for Eric and did not want his manager to feel he had been 'let down' in any way, but he also could not face playing permanently in the reserves, which was in effect the second team, for the rest of his time at Sheffield Wednesday. So, he finally decided, to 'ask the question!'

It was therefore an understandably nervous approach finally made to Taylor in an effort to verbalise his feelings and prompt a reaction from his manager. Asking for a transfer in those days was like asking to leave a job without the surety or comfort that anyone else would feel like offering you another. Tony was grateful for the opportunity provided him by Wednesday and when the discussion regarding his future finally took place, Eric Taylor told him truthfully and without any sensation that his job as manager was to provide the club with a successful team and whilst the first team he had was winning and not bogged down with injuries, then for the foreseeable future, that team would remain in place. He did not attempt to persuade Tony to stay and pointed out that although he was still young, he had unfortunately lost a few years to some of his contemporaries by the time he served in the army. However, he also knew that this talented young winger was keen to establish himself as a first team regular and made it known he would support any move Tony wished to make. The final decision then was with Tony, who really was unsure what to do in terms of developing his career. The existing choice was to stay with a good, well managed club like Wednesday and simply be patient … or move on!

CHAPTER FOUR

From a 'Minsterman' to a 'Hornet'

It was May 3rd, 1949 when the letter from Eric Taylor confirmed to Tony Collins his position on the 'transfer list'. It was a short and formal notification which read as follows.

> *Dear Sir,*
> *Further to our letter of the 29th ultimo, you have been placed on the transfer list at a fee of £750.00.*
> *Best wishes,*
> *Yours faithfully'*

The conversations that took place between the two men concerning the transfer to York are not recorded in detail and memories are distant, but the amount of £750.00 would have purchased a fairly good semi-detached house in that year and related to around £23,500.00 at today's values. So after being with the team at Wednesday for such a short period and only playing in the reserves, Tony's financial standing had been enhanced considerably. He had started with Sheffield Wednesday worth practically nothing … and now, although he didn't actually own one, he was worth a reasonable sized house!

On May 6th, an approach was made by Midland League club Peterborough United and in July by Eastern Counties club Clacton

Town. The manager of Clacton, Jimmy McLuckie advised that club players were only 'part time' but they were paid good money, a bonus and travelling expenses. This may seem to be a strange offer to a well known player with a National Football League club but it should be remembered that footballers, even the best of them, at that particular time in history, were earning a fairly meagre living and as Sir Alex Ferguson famously once indicated … 'Good players don't play for money!'

This was truly the case in 1949. Not many players owned a car and generally moved around using public transport. In the closed season, during the summer months, weekly pay would be reduced, bonuses non-existent and travelling expenses not available. As a result, most would need to attend a local 'labour exchange' to sign on for the government social payment – 'the dole'. The problem for many of them was that once signed on, if you were offered a job, you had to take it or else the 'dole money' was stopped immediately. At that time, the wages of professional footballers were limited by the Football Association and the 'retain and transfer' system ruled how players were moved from one club to another. The Professional Football Player's representative organisation had been formed in 1907 as the Association of Football Players and Trainers Union (AFPTU) to act as a trade union of sorts, representing the interests of players throughout the country. The Football Association refused to recognise the AFPTU who wished to challenge the maximum wage and transfer restrictions, and banned players affiliated with the Union. Players would have to wait until 1961 for Jimmy Hill, chairman of what had become the Professional Footballer's Association, to succeed in scrapping the maximum wage, which at that time was £20.00 per week; approximately £397.00 in today's value. It had to be understood that under the rather comfortable rules agreed by all club owners of the day, a players' life was more or less controlled completely by the club itself. A player could not leave without the consent of the chairman and manager. So, it would often be the case that if a player was refused a transfer for whatever reason, he would volunteer to become the union representative. This would be a more or less guaranteed ticket out of the club gates in very short time. No club manager wanted a union man in his team.

This was fortunately not the case with Tony Collins and within a matter of weeks from being placed on the transfer list, he had made up his mind to accept an offer from York City, a side playing in the Third Division (North) and sitting near the middle of the table at number fourteen. The manager there was Thomas 'Tom' Mitchell who had been in charge since 1937. He was an experienced 50 year old ex-player who knew the game and what he wanted from his players. His record spoke for itself making over 143 appearances for Leeds United and 60 for Newcastle United at outside left, scoring a respectable number of goals along the way.

Information surrounding the negotiated move of Tony from Sheffield Wednesday to York City is sketchy, but from Tony's point of view it was less about money and more about his ambitions for the game. Whatever Wednesday was perceived to be, it was a well managed and well facilitated club. Because of that, it was also the home of several International players. In Tony's eyes, this could well have been a block to his undaunted desire to play first team football and it was therefore understandable that he held a wish to move on and try with a team that was not so well equipped with first class players. But despite showing his paces in the reserves, in his mind, there would also be some uncertainty as to the *real* reason he was not asked to play first team football at Hillsborough. However, when the time finally came there was little doubt about the sentiment at Wednesday and when he did eventually make the move they sent him a telegram of congratulations which read ...

'Best wishes for a successful season from all at Sheffield Wednesday'

Perhaps the transfer was also in part driven by the need to finance Tony's new responsibilities in the shape of a wife and the potential of a new family. Having Edith with him was a substantial bonus as far as he was concerned. His first payslip dated August 6th, 1949 confirmed a gross wage of £8 Pounds and 10 Shillings, less £1 Pound income tax and 4 Shillings and 11 Pence for insurance. This provided him with a net of £7.00 Pounds, 5 Shillings and 1 Penny; no King's ransom by any measure but a wage for doing something he simply loved. It is worth noting that at that time, the average wage for a man in England, committing to a 40 to 48 hour working week, was £7 and 10 Shillings. So, playing football for a living could not be considered an easy route to wealth, not forgetting that for half the year, the off season, wages would be significantly reduced.

On August 10th, Tony's new manager wrote to him ...

'Dear Tony,
You are chosen in the practice match on Saturday. Please be here at 1:30 as I am taking this opportunity for a pre-season talk to all players.
Yours etc.
T. Mitchell.'

The move to York City appeared to be full of promise despite also being something of a culture shock. Facilities were not what he was used to when playing for the 'Owls' and the manager definitely 'had a different way about him'. However, except for a few limited appearances, Tony was generally held to play in the reserves despite his talent being extolled by sports writers at just about every match he played during the 1949 – 50 season. The manager's wife also did her fair share in supporting the welfare of players signed to the club and wrote to Tony on August 10th …

> *Dear Tony,*
> *I have found a very nice place for you at No. 45 Westminster Road, York. It is not far from the ground and is a very nice district. I have arranged for you to go to this house for tea on Saturday so you can arrange to stay over if you wish or make arrangements to go in on Monday.*
> *Yours sincerely,*
> *Mrs. N. Mitchell.'*

Tony's first meeting with the owners of 45 Westminster Road was to prove a fortuitous one as a positive relationship developed immediately between Tony, with his new wife Edith and the Hodgson's. Arthur Hodgson was a train driver, a very much respected profession in the day and his wife Rose worked at the famous 'Rowntree' confectionery factory in York. Tony recalls that this outgoing couple became like an aunt and uncle to him and Edith and although they did not realize it at the time, their bond of friendship would last the rest of their lives. After the move from York, the Collins family visited the Hodgson's regularly and a very young Sarita, Tony's daughter, recalls the large and tempting selection of misshapen biscuits and odd sized chocolate regularly made available for hungry children on the kitchen table … and always offered with a smile. There was much banter between the particularly London accented Tony and the very Yorkshire intoned Rose Hodgson. In true Yorkshire style, her vowels were often extended and sentences drawn and Tony would joke with her about it.

'Leg pulling' was the order of the day at Westminster Road in late 1949 and early 1950 and these were considered by Tony and Edith to be very happy days. One thing that stood out about the Hodgson family for this young 23 year old York City football player was the lack of interest in his background and origins. To the social circle he was introduced to by Arthur and Rose, he was simply a 'bloody southerner' and someone Arthur was proud to take with him to the social club and pubs that all the other train drivers took a drink in. He was known as a 'cheekie chappie' and once again, his personality and quick wittedness enabled him to mix easily with people and generally command their respect.

Things were going well then for Tony off the pitch … but what about on it. The signing of Tony Collins as York's new left winger was heralded by the local newspapers with a large picture of the signing event showing Tony with pen to paper and manager Tom Mitchell looking on. However, the pictures that followed revealed their new star signing actually playing in the reserves. That of course did not stop the sports reporters from unidentified newspapers of the day reminding everyone what a catch they had.

> *'Collins was there to head into the back of the net with bullet-like force!'*
> *'Collins, back at left half, made judicious use of the ball with shrewd passes ...'*
> *'York were the more aggressive and with Collins an outstanding forward ...'*
> *'Many team selections continue to reach this office. G.H.E. advocates the inclusion of Collins for his consistent good play ...'*

Finally, the words of encouragement from the local and National press would make little difference in any decision to play Tony Collins as a full time member of the first team and this final quote, penned after he had left for Watford, simply says it all!

'Meanwhile it is rather ironical that players discarded by York are doing well elsewhere, notably Tony Collins who is attracting attention at outside left for Watford.'

York City started the 1949/50 season at number 14 in the Third Division (North) league, but would end it with only 31 points out of 42 games and languishing at the very bottom. Manager, Tom Mitchell, would resign and retire to set up a family sports outfitting shop in York. He would also later become a director of the club. Dick Duckworth would take over the reins for the next two years dragging York back to number 17 in the 1950/51 season and number 10 by the end of the season in 1952.

From Tony's viewpoint, whatever thoughts he may have had about his position and time spent at Bootham Crescent, his manager Tom Mitchell was regarded by himself and all other members of the team and staff at York City as a gentleman. His replacement with Dick Duckworth however, was the final push Tony needed to make a move south. His memories of the man are of an uncouth individual whom some would describe as literally a 'madman' with a 'hit and hope' attitude to the playing of 'the beautiful game'. A phrase had been coined by Rugby fans at the time stating that soccer was a game for gentlemen, played by hooligans, and it appeared that Duckworth was out to prove this to be the case. To his mind, football was not necessarily a game of skill and flair and he often made his point if things were not going well with physical displays of his mood. He was also not shy of offering personal comment about individuals and their shortcomings from his rather biased point of view. As a result, the opportunity to make some uncalled for statements relating to the colour of a person's skin could often not be resisted. Tony did not like him; did not feel comfortable working with him and therefore confirmed in his own mind that a discreet exit from the Bootham Crescent ground would be his most positive plan.

Would York City and its ill tempered, foul mouthed manager be prepared to let him go? It appears to be the case, but the treatment Tony had received in his short time under Duckworth had significantly knocked his confidence as he moved back to his home in London and to people who loved and cherished him. Duckworth did in fact recommend the talents of Tony Collins to the manager at Watford and it appears no money would exchange hands with regard to the transaction if the young ambitious player wanted to go. Edith stayed in Sheffield with her family and the parting was a strained and anxious period for the newly-weds. However, this was not the time to dwell on failure; Tony Collins was looking for success ... but he might have to move permanently back south to find it.

~~~~

The signing to Watford Football Club for the 1950/51 season was inspired by many feelings, some of which were possibly related to the state of the game he loved, his place in it as a fit and talented professional sportsman and a desire to better the life of his family. Edith had remained his rock and totally supportive of the move 'South' if it meant Tony would be able to further his so far unspectacular career. From her family home at 316, Halifax Road in Sheffield, on August 9th she wrote ...

'Hope you are well and your foot is a lot better. I suppose they will be keen on your training now with Saturday fast approaching for the trial match ... I am sure we shall be happy once we are settled, which I hope will be soon.'

Watford, a Third Division club playing in the Southern section was sensibly placed at 6th in the league with 45 points from 42 games at the end of the 1950 season. The manager, Eddie Hapgood was an ex-Arsenal and England player who wrote one of the very first football autobiographies in 1945 titled 'Football Ambassadors'. However, he was to leave after only two seasons and his place was taken by Ron Gray. He was a 30 year old North Shields born pragmatist who could perhaps be considered unfortunate in overseeing the fall of the club's fortunes and forced to watch them end up bottom of the league in 1951. This meant having to engage in the embarrassing process of applying to the rest of the league members to actually stay in the Third Division.

The system of playing divisions agreed at the start-up of the league again after WWII was to still have a First and Second Division and two Third Division competitions, catering for the North and South of the country. In effect, there was nowhere for a team to go if it was unfortunate enough to end up at the bottom of either of the Third Divisions. However, each Division needed to hold a minimum number of teams to allow the whole league system to function, so the simple ruling was made to allow the bottom four clubs to apply for re-election to the League and naturally, no one would be turned down. However, for a manager and the members of a team, the process was one of some discomfort and could trigger a decline in the support of fans, whose weekly turnstile patronage paid everyone's wages.

Things were therefore not good at the Vicarage Road ground and the 1950/51 season for Tony Collins would be something of a baptism of fire. He would also see two more managers in charge at Watford before moving on. Ron Gray would be replaced by Haydn Green, a 64 year old who would only last one season and then Len Goulden, a 40 year old Londoner undertaking his first managerial role and someone who would be in a more settled residence from 1952 to 1955.

Under a fractured and regularly changing managerial philosophy, during his time with Watford from 1950 to the end of the season in 1953, Tony Collins would go on to make 90 appearances for the first team and be credited with 8 goals. He would also make a lifelong friend in fellow player Frank Jackett, a Welshman with an ebullient character and fine wing half whose son Kenny also played for Watford and would eventually end up becoming manager. The last player contract that Tony would sign at Watford before leaving in 1953 would be for a wage of £10.0.0 per week during the playing season from August 1st 1952 to May 2nd 1953 and £8.0.0 per week from May until June. He would also be paid £2.0.0 extra when playing for the first team. In the winter of 1951, Tony and Edith would move into their first real house together, a rented bungalow called The Spinney in Dawes Lane, Sarratt, a small village just outside Watford. This would end the regular separations and short periods in 'digs' at 90 Kings Avenue, Watford and a short spell back to his home at 396 Portobello Road.

Although the administrative situation at Watford left much to be desired with an unsettling change of manager year upon year, for Tony it was a time to shine. Not only was he now a regular first team player, others had their eye on this charismatic character known to have an ability to create goals from very little. An unidentified national newspaper of the day reported:

Official eye on Collins — *'It looks as though Watford's Tony Collins stands a good chance of playing in a representative game before the season is out. I understand that an F.A. selector went to Aylesbury on Saturday for the express purpose of watching Collins in action.'*

This was a surprising situation of course. The question had to be asked why the FA selectors would want to watch a player in a third division club. Surely, if they were not good enough to play in the first division, they would not be good enough for the English team ... would they? Every newspaper pundit could see it; all of Tony's team mates at Watford could see it and the FA said they wanted to see it ... so why was a black man with the talent of Tony Collins not chosen to play football for England? Perhaps the answer is in the question?

Another comment regarding the 'scouting' of Collins also from an unidentified newspaper and during his Watford days stated:

> Can Watford resist it? – *'Watford's stylish outside left, Tony Collins, is attracting the attention of First Division scouts. Though Chairman Rigby Taylor says "We are not selling Tony" both Burnley and Sunderland are convinced that a big cheque will prove too strong an inducement for Watford to refuse.'*

So, Watford's new signing, Tony Collins, was playing some exciting football and keeping the fans happy as the teams overall pitch performance improved. League position also rocketed, seeing Watford rise from 23 in the Third Division (South) to position number 10 at the end of the 1953 season. With such a pedigree, such dedication to the game and such interest by other, wealthier clubs in the First Division, Tony was still playing Third Division football ... and there had to be many around him who were truly unsure as to the reason why. Perhaps with the benefit of hindsight, the reason someone with his skill-set and character was not getting the recognition he deserved was simply down to his colour.

The newshounds were correct in saying Sunderland had a

confirmed interest in acquiring Tony but ebullient chairman of Watford, Rigby Taylor, said publicly that '£12,500.00 would not buy him' so they went and bought Billy Elliot from Burnley. Tony raised the possibility that if the amount Taylor was talking about was his true value, then he surely must be worth a 'benefit match', but Watford would not guarantee him one. So when he eventually made the move to Norwich City, the fee obtained was considered by many as a joke compared to the chairman's earlier boast.

The skilful play of Watford's new winger had not gone unnoticed by the national selectors and England manager Walter Winterbottom, someone who would eventually be knighted for his services to the Football League. He started as the very first manager of the England football team and remained so from 1946 to 1962. The name of Tony Collins was being talked about and Winterbottom attended a midweek evening match to see the man in action. However, the rain was relentless, the pitch heavy and conditions described as a mud-bath. It proved difficult to run with the ball, make accurate passes or receive service on the wing from team players in the middle of the park. Opportunities to shine were few and overall it was a disappointing night for Tony with the prospect of the England team bringing on-board its first black player to compete at senior level buried for some years to come. In fact not until some 27 years later would Viv Anderson take to the field for England under the watchful eye of Ron Greenwood in a 1-0 win against Czechoslovakia at Wembley. His comment some years after the match was: ...

'It was a big thing at the time. There were not many black lads playing at the top level, so I can see why people made a fuss about it!'

If 'people made a fuss about it' then in 1978 ... imagine what kind of 'fuss' would have been made in 1951. Looking back on the period and the opportunities for black people in general, some would say that being a top level black footballer at the time could be equated to being openly 'gay' today in that no one would be sure how the fans would react and how such a person would affect the atmosphere in the dressing room. The mantra of the time in the boardrooms of first class English Football could possibly have been … 'No need to upset the apple-cart!'

Tony himself would perhaps look back at some future stage and put this period of his life under some further scrutiny. However, as a professional football player he knew he would soon be looking thirty in the face and if he was to ever break into the big time, he would need to 'get his skates on!' There were also the ambitions for his family to consider and he and Edith needed to feel more settled than they were at Watford in order to kick-start the process. So he made the decision to leave the club, not ever thinking he would actually be back there within a few short years, even if it was only for a brief period.

However, not forgetting what was happening on the pitch, what about Tony and Edith's private life at that rather unsettling period? Tony was initially offered a house in West Watford that he didn't like and then he found the Sarratt bungalow style property that he and Edith definitely did like. It was actually a semi-detached property and their next door neighbours were George and Mary, who they got along with famously. A trout stream ran at the bottom of the garden and in this idyllic setting, by the early part of 1953, Tony and Edith were expecting their first child. Unfortunately, the baby was premature and did not survive and this setback took some getting over by them both.

The closed season work necessity was again a problem quickly solved by finding some at the nearby garden centre. The owners were glad to have a very fit young man on the books for the busy summer period and Tony enjoyed the work and interaction with staff and customers alike.

The 'game' at Watford continued with the fans telling it as they saw it. If Tony missed what they regarded as a 'sitter' then they would shout 'Get back to your barrow ... barrow boy!' making reference to the part of London he came from; the Portobello Road. There would of course be abuse relating to his colour but as he was a popular player, at Watford such occasions were thankfully few and far between.

One small but amusing aside relating to his time at Watford was the day that Frank Jackett, a team player, needed to go to the dentist. Frank was the father of Kenny Jackett who would go on to become a successful club manager after playing for Watford, making 337 appearances and putting away 25 goals. Frank was a typical Welshman and suffered from a strong accent that was difficult to understand. He was a great character but his fear of all things medical was well known and when the appointment was finally made for Frank's trip to the dentist, he asked Tony to go along with him for a bit of moral support. Seemingly the dentist had Frank in the chair and a finger in his mouth pushing against the troublesome tooth. He asked the standard question: 'Alright?' The next thing Tony heard as he waited outside for Frank to reappear was a loud scream. It was the dentist. He retracted his bruised finger from Frank's mouth asking 'What on earth did you do that for you silly sod?' Frank replied: 'Oh ... I really am sorry. I thought you said bite!'

The decision made by Collins to leave the club caused a bit of a storm amongst the supporters and the local press. They liked him, there was no doubting that. He played with a certain 'style' that was considered attractive, entertaining and resulted in goals being scored. In a match against Brighton where Watford won 2–1, they were called 'plodders' except for comments about Tony.

'Reward came their way when, a quarter-hour from the end, Collins, this most stylish wing forward on the field, equalised'

In a match against Leyton Orient where Watford scraped home with a 1–0 win the comment was:

'Watford's outside left Collins, was once again the best man on the field …'

A match report (from an unidentified newspaper of the day) where Watford trounced Walsall 3–0 was titled:

Collins and Halves star for Watford – *'Collins did much as he liked at outside left and it was from one of his accurate centres that Reid opened Watford's score in the ninth minute'*

In a letter to an unidentified local newspaper of the day, a supporter noted as a Mr L. Jerrad wrote …

'I believe in leaving team management to the team manager, but I do hope that the club will continue to play Collins at inside forward.'

So when the news broke that Tony was on the move from Watford, there were concerns amongst the fans and the sporting commentators of the day. During the 52-53 season Watford had managed to climb back up to 10th position in the league, claiming 47 points from 46 games but the aspirations of the supporters appeared to be much higher than that. Therefore, any suggestion of a move by one their most charismatic players would be questioned and such concerns given many column inches of exposure before the move took place.

The headline was: *'Collins: 'Bids Please,' To Top Clubs'* with the sub-headline being *'No Club row – just a player's ambition. Will the news that Watford have agreed to Tony Collins' request for a transfer bring a spate of offers? And, if it does, what sort of price will the clubs place on this immaculate master of the touchline?'*

Further extracts from this long report (made by an unidentified newspaper and reporter of the day) stated that: *'Whilst the directors are very reluctant to let him go, if an offer is received which is acceptable to the Board, they will not stand in his way'*

It went on to confirm that Tony's point of view was of course, understandable. At 25 years of age he was at the peak of his form and he probably felt that 'now was the time to act' if he was to satisfy his ambitions. The speculation did not, by necessity, last very long as Tony Collins needed to earn a living, start a family and move on with his career. Moves in those days did not take much time once a decision had been made simply because being a professional football player was not necessarily an easy life. To get on in the game, a player had to always be prepared to make a move otherwise it was possible to lose out on money relating to transfer terms. No one really knew how long they would stay with a particular club, especially if a player's worth was on the rise. Players were bought and sold as a commodity and high transfer prices were what made a club wealthy. However, the expected First Division club interest in Tony did not materialise as everyone around him had hoped for … and had cause to expect. A decision needed to be made and the press announcement in an unidentified local newspaper of the day was a short one.

Norwich Sign New Left Winger – *'Norwich City have signed Tony Collins, Watford left winger for a fee in the region of £5,000.00. A former*

Sheffield Wednesday and York City player, Collins missed only one League match for Watford last year.'

The announcement was interesting in that no one had asked Tony how much his transfer fee was and his recollection of the amount was only £3,500.00. In the day before 'agents' were employed to act on behalf of individual footballers, a player had to manage his own affairs and some of the younger ones had their fathers representing them at any negotiations with club management. A player was the one to put himself on the transfer list and was also the one to negotiate his financial situation, including the bonus, which was calculated as a percentage of the full transfer fee. In most cases, the standard would be around 10% and in the move from York to Watford, Tony personally received £100.00. On the move from Watford to Norwich, the amount was £300.00. It was also not unusual for players to receive an extra sum commonly recognised as a signing on bonus of sorts.

The move to Carrow Road, home of Norwich City, was finally confirmed in a contract dated June 30th, 1953 providing £10.0.0 a week during the summer months, £12.0.0 a week (£280.00 at today's value) during the season and a £2.0.0 extra payment when playing in the League Team. The transfer fee would be worth around £115,000.00 at today's values and was considered to be worthy of the man. With some extra money perhaps burning a hole in his pocket, Tony had his eye on a nice new Jaguar motor car and Edith was all for him buying it … but, once again 'a sensible head on sensible shoulders' dictated that the money was better off in his bank account than invested in an extravagant set of wheels.

CHAPTER FIVE

The Canaries, the Gulls and the Eagles!

Norman Harvey Low was the 39 year old manager of Norwich City, named by its fans as 'The Canaries.' He was born in Scotland, became a professional footballer and was also the son of Scottish International player Wilf Low. He had led the club to second place in the Third Division South ratings during the 1950–51 season but missed out on promotion to the Second Division. Low was a man with a firm desire to oversee the promotion of the club and felt he needed to bring some experience to the team.

The signing of Tony Collins was considered by Low to be a good move for the club … but for Tony, it proved to be a bad one. The club had access to money and with Alf Caston being not only one of the directors but also a successful local builder; he was able to ensure that club owned houses were made available to Norwich City players. Tony moved into his very first 'club' house with Edith. It was brand new and gave the pair the kind of morale boost they needed to be convinced that Tony's career was 'on the way up!' There was also a double celebration on November 7th of that year with Edith reaching the fetching age of 30 and Norwich beating Arsenal in a cup-tie match.

Norwich was a somewhat strange club for the time, languishing in the Third Division but with money and ambition enough to power them to the very heart of First Division football. It should be remembered that training a football team in 1953 was down more to assurances required regarding fitness than any educational route to the tactics of the game; beating the opponent with set play moves, communication on the field of play and most importantly understanding the differing talents of differing players in differing positions. From a tactical point of view, Tony thought Norwich had simply lost the plot. However, as many other teams played a fairly undisciplined and 'hit and hope' kind of football, any shortcomings at Norwich City were not immediately visible. Players held fixed positions consisting of a forward line with a Centre Forward, Inside Right, Inside Left, Outside Right and Outside Left. The centre of the field was to be swept and marshalled by a Centre Half, Left Half and Right Half. The defence line consisted of a Left Back and a Right Back (the Full Backs) with the final stopping power invested in a Goal Keeper.

At Norwich, with Collins playing at Outside Left, a natural position for a left footed player, there was little or no plan of play with the full backs simply intent on banging the ball as far up front as possible and away from them and their goal. No one seemed to understand the value of a fast, sure footed winger who should have been part of a build-up of play that could circumnavigate a tough defence and gain open access to the goal mouth.

This basic policy of 'brute force and ignorance' was even further advanced by an announcement in 1954 that Norwich had decided only to play 6ft tall players. Tony at a healthy five foot, ten and a half inches fell somewhat short of this specification and therefore knew his time with the 'Canaries' was probably coming to an end.

Due to the tall players debacle, he only made 29 first team appearances in the two seasons from 1953 to 1955 and was credited with only two goals. On the brighter side, being a first team player, he had access to FA Cup Final tickets at Wembley and this was to become a looked forward to annual pilgrimage along with an opportunity to catch up with the London side of the Collins family. However, a fully pregnant Edith would be unable to make the 1954 event and instead made May of that year even more memorable by giving birth to Tony and Edith's first child. The date was May 4th and the child was a baby girl who would be called Sandra Elaine. Another significant event in the July of 1954 was the ending of all rationing in the UK. This was to be a celebrated change in everyone's lives and signalled the realisation that the country could now begin to breathe again with better opportunities just round the corner.

Of course, the problem of what to do in the closed season to 'make ends meet' was always looming large. At Norwich, Tony quickly found some work on building sites digging out cess pits for the previously mentioned director of the club, Alf Caston. This was energetic work in that the lower the digging, the higher the soil had to be thrown. Tony recalls an old guy regularly labouring on site whose name was Joe. He had an unusual American style accent having spent many years working in the North American Yukon. Joe had many tales to tell, some of them tall and others not so tall. Tony would help with large barrow loads of cement needing to be pushed across precarious plank ramps. The boss on site was nicknamed 'bullet' and he told Tony, if he ever wanted a full time job, there would be one waiting for him. The work that Tony did in the closed season served two purposes: making up the difference of reduced wages and keeping him physically fit so that when the season started again, he was … ready to go!

A move to Torquay United was one welcomed by Collins. He had a good feeling about the club and its manager, 36 year old Eric Webber, who had been with the club at its Plainmoor ground since 1951.

He was an ex-player making 182 senior appearances for Southampton and 149 for Torquay United. In the January of 1955, the season before Tony joined; he took the club to an historic 4-0 win over the much superior Leeds United in the English FA Cup and then lost out narrowly in a 1-0 defeat against First Division Huddersfield Town. The official attendance at that particular game was nearly 22,000 and still remains the Club record.

Although arriving fit and well at Torquay, the famous 'bracing air' of the English Riviera was seemingly having an effect on Tony. It was a strange and unwelcome effect ... and nothing to do with his level of fitness. In fact he was sure he had contracted some form of sleeping sickness. His whole metabolism was in a confused state and he felt permanently tired with heavy legs and aching muscles. This was initially worrying to both Tony and Edith but fortunately, after a few weeks, this worrying physical phenomenon began to wear off and he slowly regained his normally robust fitness levels.

The 'Gulls' were in a good place sitting at number five in the Third Division (South) and destined to rise to second in the 56–57 season, prior to league re-structuring and just missing out on promotion to the Second Division by goal average. There was also a certain level of satisfaction for Tony Collins when playing his old club Norwich into the ground with a 7–1 defeat ... with others to follow. The Chairman and his family were completely immersed in the game and on one occasion when chasing the top spot in the league, Tony recalls the Chairman's wife coming into the dressing room to advise the players very bluntly she 'had some money she didn't want!', suggesting that for a winning performance, everyone could expect a bonus! She was much admired at the club and one day she bumped into Tony and Edith with the baby in town. 'There's no question whose daughter she is' would be the comment, although efforts to produce another child had sadly ended up in disappointment. Edith had needed to be rushed to hospital in the early stages of pregnancy resulting in the unfortunate loss of her baby and from that day on Tony held a view that something had gone wrong there. However, in the middle fifties' enquiries regarding the competence of the National Health Service were not welcome and the whole business was shrouded in secrecy. So, not much change there then!

This setback for both was fortunately replaced with great joy when Andrew Peter Collins entered the world on July 25th, 1956. The family unit was now considered complete; a successful career, a happy working life in a beautiful part of the country and a small boy and girl to provide them both with endless pleasure. Tony Collins could not be happier and visitors Kit, Wilfred and Sarah Murdoch arrived in Torquay to see what they regarded as their grandchildren … and spend a few days by the seaside.

One of the bonuses of living and working in Torquay was of course the weather and the seaside location. Although the house they lived in was a 'club owned' property, Tony and Edith ran a successful bed and breakfast business from it to add a little extra to the coffers and make up for the closed season wage dilemma. The children were not only spoilt at home but also by the local traders. Rationing had ended a few years before but the nation was still trying to get back on its feet financially. When baby Sandra Collins accompanied her footballer father to the local butchers shop, a big smile would result in an extra row of 'free' sausages somehow finding their way into the bag. Both Tony and Edith loved the house in Torquay and Edith became a keen gardener.

The team trainer lived next door and his little 8 or 9 year old girl would often ask Tony if he thought it was likely to snow that year? She, of course, had never seen snow due to the gentle and mild 'Riviera' climate they lived in.

Life in the West Country was conducted at a much slower pace than Watford or Norwich and certainly much less hectic than London. One day, Tony chased after the window cleaner who he had forgotten to pay for a couple of weeks only to be told "Don't worry Mr Collins, I'll get it from you next week". It was a different way of life completely and many of the team players voted for a game of golf in the afternoons. As a result, a few players each year became addicted, eventually leaving their soccer career behind for the captivating sport.

The press however, liked Torquay's new winger and made suitable comment in an unidentified local newspaper of the day:

Shock Goals Gave Torquay Lucky Points – *'Two shock goals by Collins the Torquay inside left, in the seventh and eighth minute of Saturday's game at Vicarage Road, gave the United two points they scarcely deserved. Collins first goal came when he consummated a move he had started himself in midfield ...'*

In a match against Millwall where Torquay unfortunately lost 3-2, comments from local sports reporters were still being made about the performance of Tony Collins on the pitch.

'Both Ron Shaw and Tony Collins, the Torquay wingers, played well. Their centres brought plenty of work for Finlayson in goal. This pair were mainly responsible for the revival of Torquay ... they were always in the Millwall half, pushing and chipping over passes ...'

However, the reduced tempo proved difficult for an ambitious Collins, a regime which more or less consisted of enforced relaxation mixed with a necessary requirement for bursts of high physical and mental energy on the football pitch. It was a difficult situation for Tony to get his head round but it didn't affect the great relationship he had with Eric Webber and they used to chat a lot about football in general and tactics in particular. Perhaps it was as a result of these conversations that Tony began to think more about a career move into coaching and management. By some, it could have been considered a natural change of direction but the actual decision itself was a couple of years away. His priority at that particular moment was to work at getting Torquay into the Second Division.

So, what was it that eventually saw Tony make a move back to Watford? Was it the disappointment at not making it out of the Third Division on something as technical as goal average? The fight was with Ipswich Town. Both teams had played 46 matches and collected 59 points but only one team at that time could be promoted up to the next level and the decider in this case was down to goal average. Ipswich held on to an average of 1.87 and Torquay could only manage 1.39. It was a heartbreaking situation for the club, the manager, the directors and most importantly, the fans. There was no shame therefore in Tony Collins accepting an approach to move back to Watford who were sitting nearly in the middle of the league table and needing a bit of a 'shove' before becoming a possible victim of the new arrangements for the Football League system that would come into force fully for the 1958-59 season. Under this newly agreed arrangement, there would be four divisions with the Third Divisions North and South combining to make up a new Third and Fourth Division.

The press managed to grab a hold of the situation and on June 14th, 1957 the *West Herts and Watford Observer* put out the following unaccredited article.

Watford Bid For Torquay To Accept – He May Rejoin The Blues Next Week – *'Tony Collins, Watford's former left winger may be coming back to Vicarage Road! Watford completed negotiations with Torquay for his transfer this week …'*

The reporter went on to confirm that Torquay were anxious to keep him, but Collins wanted to make the move leaving Watford to open negotiations. He added the comment:

'Collins was a popular figure during his first stay at Vicarage Road and his return should be welcomed by supporters who remember his clever footwork and accurate centres'

Tony Collins had served Torquay United well making 89 registered appearances and scoring 17 accredited goals in two playing seasons. The reason for his need to make a move was explained to Webber as being one of family. He was at heart a 'London boy' needing to get back to familiar accents and more regular access to people that really mattered to him. He was now a 'family man' with two small children to care for and he felt at that time the place to be was somewhere near London.

Eric Webber did not want Tony to leave and he made it very clear. He told him that if he hadn't been going home, there was no way he would have been allowed to leave United. However, a transfer was agreed and a fee paid, putting a little bit more money into the Collins family coffers. One other friendship that was to last for many years was that forged with Don Mills who was an established first team player and someone who had stayed the course for ten years, making over 300 appearances. Don was the person who introduced Tony and Edith to the delights of holidaying in Cornwall and Newquay in particular. The whole of the Collins family would spend many happy days there over the next 50 years leaving them all with very special memories of this very unique part of England. Tony used to refer to it as "God's country", and often commented that if he came out of the game he would be satisfied being a postman living there. The West Country was a place where just for a couple of weeks each year he was completely removed from the game of football, and revelled in being the playful family man, spending endless hours on the beach at Crantock and Watergate Bay with Edith and the children.

When they first went to Watergate Bay there was an ex-RAF building for officers cut into the cliff. Tony and Edith often commented it would make a smashing hotel, and in years to come it would eventually be converted to become The Watergate Bay Hotel. This then is where the family would stay for their holidays from the 1980s onwards. Up to that point it would be the first week in a caravan at Disley's caravan site in Crantock and then the luxury of a flat next to the stables, overlooking Trenance boating lake for the second week.

The order of the day would be up and out, a route march to the beach, carrying a windbreaker, mallet, swim suits, towels, buckets and spades, fishing net (for the rock pools) a flask, the obligatory football oh and don't forget the kids! There would be a lunch break from the blazing sun, enjoyed at the Seagull Pub in Crantock, or if some kind soul would stay on the beach with the kids, then it would be a swift few glasses of scrumpy in the Albion pub, opposite the Seagull, (a place where children were not allowed), and a Cornish Pasty to provide sustenance for the afternoons sporting fixtures! This would most likely be beach cricket, racing in rubber rings down the Gannel River, long jump, football skills and a knock about with anyone who wanted a game. Tony may have been London's long jump champion, but Edith was to prove more than skilful enough to be declared the hop, skip and jump champion!

~~~~

Tony's tenure back at Watford was a short one. Vicarage Road had been taken over by a new manager in the form of Neil McBain, a 62 year old Scotsman who was perhaps past his prime in management terms. He was an ex-player of reasonable success at wing-half and had been player-manager at Watford from 1929 to 1937.

Tony and Neil did not really get on and Tony comments that "… his office was always a mess with fish and chip papers all over the desk and he was quite a foul man. He never did anything with the players on the pitch …" Had he made the wrong move?… from a friendly well managed club at the heart of what England regarded as its very own Riviera, back to a Vicarage Road that was nearly unrecognizable compared to the place Tony had left, only four years previously.

Fortunately, things were to change quite quickly for this frustrated fleet footed winger who was desperate to play good quality football. On the occasions that Watford played against Crystal Palace, the Palace manager, Cyril Spiers, always took some time out to find Tony and have a few words after the game. Tony felt he was being assessed by Cyril who was in charge of a generally young team. He wanted, and probably needed, an experienced player to add to his young squad and with persistence managed to lever the 31 year old away from the clutches of Neil McBain.

Tony joined the south London club, Crystal Place, nicknamed the 'Eagles' at their Selhurst Park ground for the 1957-58 season. This was probably one of the best moves Tony had made up to that date and with the 'Palace' he was to be at his most productive, securing 14 accredited goals out of 55 appearances. The move involved another transfer fee of course and another payment to Tony, which was more than welcome. Not only was he now playing for a club with a bit of 'zip' in it, and ambitions to climb quickly out of the 'basement' of league football in the Fourth Division, Tony was close to his beloved London and all the proud members of his extended family.

The contract signed with Crystal Palace provided for a wage of £14.0.0 a week in the playing season, with a bonus of £3.0.0 for first team appearances and £12.0.0 a week in the off season. The press took note of Tony's arrival when reporting a crucial match against Exeter in which Palace won 1-0 and these are extracts from unaccredited reports in unidentified newspapers of the day.

'After seventy five minutes Collins roamed down on the left wing and crossed the ball to the opposite flank. Right winger Bernard Harrison moved calmly into an unmarked position, controlled the ball perfectly and hammered a shot to the roof of the net'

In a match report where Johnny Byrne was featured, the donation to a 4–1 winning score-line by Tony was not missed.

'A dodging run … a fierce shot. Russell Crossley could only parry. Tony Collins later to link up splendidly with Byrne, was on the spot … and Palace were one up'

When Collins was out of the team with an injury, the press were keen to show their concern with the following piece.

Palace Hope To Have Collins Back – *'Tony Collins is almost certain to return to the Crystal Palace team at outside-left for the return game with Queen's Park Rangers at Shepherd's Bush on Saturday.'*

A note was made that Collins was injured at Newport on Easter Saturday and had missed the last three games. *'He will play if he is fit'* Manager Cyril Spiers commented. *'Collins has finished treatment but did not join in the practice …'*

Fitness was a key element of strategy at Crystal Palace and the squad were often sent off on some long cross country runs. This generated a certain level of banter amongst the participants with the younger lads often making some rude remarks about the stamina of the older players. Tony would regularly team up with one of them and the pair would 'take on' the younger lads, particularly the very talented 17 year old Jonny Byrne, by getting out in front, slowing down for a taunting catch-up and then speeding up again. Johnny would often remark about Tony's physical stamina with quips such as 'You're not human mate!'

During Tony's time at Crystal Palace, one of the players named Jimmy Sanders was an efficient midfielder who played for the Palace from 1955 to 1960. He was from a travelling family and his folk owned and worked fun fairs. However he managed it, he was always flush with cash but some of the other guys in the team would often make it a bit awkward for him because of his background. Cyril Spiers had signed him and knew his worth. Tony thought he was 'a smashing lad' and very tough on the field. He was Bristol born and had a strong West Country accent. On one occasion the Palace were due to play Charlton Athletic. Jimmy Seed, the Charlton manager of the day knew and liked Tony, but not when they were playing against him. Jimmy Sanders would occasionally suffer from terrible migraines and it affected him so badly, on occasions he would hardly be able to see. Unfortunately, on that particular day Jimmy suffered from an attack but didn't want to tell the boss. He was almost afraid of being left out of the team and losing his place. Tony picked up on what was happening and asked him if he was OK, advising him to tell the boss. Jimmy replied with a firm 'No!' and as he was playing left midfield Tony resolved to try and get him through the game if he could. He took Jimmy aside and told him that as soon as he got possession of the ball to roll it onto him, and that was the agreement.

Charlton had switched around players to ensure that Tony was heavily marked and as soon as the ball arrived at Jimmy's feet, he laid it off to Tony. A Charlton player came straight through him, kicking him badly and leaving Tony to land on the hard surfaced running track that surrounded the pitch.

The worried Palace manager, Cyril Spiers came over to him and asked if he was OK and whether or not he wanted to carry on. Tony told him through gritted teeth that he was fine. There was no way he wanted to go off; there was some revenge to be had. Tony re-confirmed to Jimmy that when he received the ball he was to pass it on. Within minutes Tony had the ball at his feet again and the same player with another wild challenge lunged at him, but Tony was prepared with some quick footwork that saw the opposition bruiser sliding across the grass on his back having missed his target completely. The humiliation continued each time Tony gained possession of the ball and the crowd had picked up on this personal battle, cheering and shouting at every twist and turn. After about 30 minutes of this the Charlton player went down feigning injury enabling him to switch to the other side of the pitch where he could take it easy. However, even his own team mates and supporters turned on him as it was obvious what was happening. Crystal Palace went on to win the game, and Jimmy made through about 75 minutes of it before coming off.

On the following Monday morning after training, Tony returned home to see a rather large and luxurious child's pram on the door step.

He asked Edith where it was from and she said one of the players had dropped it off for Sandra. It was of course from Jimmy as a sign of appreciation for Tony looking out for him during the match and naturally Tony told him he didn't have to do that ... but Jimmy said that he wanted to, so that was that!

~~~~

Tony made the move to Rochdale A.F.C. for the 1959-60 season. The manager who had recently taken charge was Jack Marshall. He had started his football career as a player for Burnley in 1936. He moved on to being a coach, joining Sheffield Wednesday in 1954 and assisting the National team manager, Walter Winterbottom with the England second team. The player contract on offer with Rochdale allowed for a weekly wage of £14.0.0 with an extra £3.0.0 bonus for first team matches.

For a 33 year old Tony Collins, it was another transfer fee and an opportunity to 'stay in the game!' During his previous year with Crystal Palace, he had obtained his preliminary certificate for coaching and he knew that this was to be the way forward. On September 24th, 1958, the Football Association awarded the qualification noting that for the 'Practical Performance' part of the examination, Mr Collins would be 'Exempt'.

Rochdale is a working class area of Greater Manchester and its football team had been active since 1907. Joining the Football League in 1921 their only real claim to any form of distinction was playing in the League Cup final of 1962 ... and it was to be Tony Collins who would guide them there. The club was the first from the bottom league division to play in the Cup final where they unfortunately lost to a rather superior and fully prepared Norwich City.

There was some level of satisfaction for the Collins family when they found themselves having to settle in Rochdale. Their rented accommodation, a substantial semi detached house at 54 Edenfield Road, was owned by a Mrs Taylor, who lived next door at number 52. After a while, Mrs Taylor revealed to Tony that she and her sons would like to sell. This news arrived on the desk of Rochdale chairman Freddie Ratcliffe who had an idea to buy both number 52 and 54 as club houses. However, Mrs Taylor had lived next to Tony and Edith for a couple of years by the time a decision was required and she told the club she would only sell to the Collins couple if they wanted it. The two families had become close and Mrs Taylor received many kindnesses from Tony and Edith during that time. Unbeknown to Edith, Tony did the deal to buy number 54 on the basis that the responsibilities of owning a property would perhaps bring to an end the wanderings of the past ten years and if something happened to Tony, Edith and the kids would have the house.

Edith was not initially impressed with his actions and although she really liked the house, she 'hit the roof' stating … 'I knew you'd go and do something like that!' Edith felt at the time that owning a property may become a millstone round their necks in the event of making another move, but that was precisely Tony's point. The family needed a base and the ages the children were at required them to be settled in their schools and making their own friends. Tony would also be spending more and more time scouting for players and travelling the country to watch football matches which for the Rochdale club was to become quite central as things were to pan out.

The Collins family were living in a slightly precarious world and reliant upon a precarious game of football to pay all the bills. Indeed, things were uncertain at Rochdale and in 1960 Jack Marshall decided that his position as manager was not a good fit and moved down the road to Blackburn Rovers, a well performing First Division side sitting at eighth in the table. This left a gap at Rochdale for a manager and an opportunity that the players felt Tony should not allow to pass him by. The lads told him "We think you should put in for it – you'll walk it!" and so he did, with the comfort of knowing he had the full backing of the team.

1 — Tony and the Army Team — 1944

2 — Army duty — Italy

3 — Beach-ball for fun

4 — Married on August 6th 1949

5 — A happy couple

6 — Wilfrid & Kit

7 — Tony and Edith — the good times

8 — Signing for York City

9 — The Watford Boys

10 — Walking out at Watford

11 — With Elton John

12 — Watford Team - 1953

13 — On the pitch

14 — Torquay United - 1957

15 — Torquay training days

16 — Keeping an eye on the ball

PART TWO

The Long Distance Runner

CHAPTER SIX

A New Life at 'The Dale'

There was nothing pretentious about the 'nickname' of Rochdale A.F.C. It was simply shortened to 'The Dale' and for the 1960-61 season Tony Collins was made player-manager at the Spotland ground, a facility on Willbutts Lane, Rochdale and built exclusively for the team in 1920. It had a standard crowd capacity of just over 10,000 but was not generally well attended.

Rochdale was never a wealthy club in terms of being a profit making organisation. In fact cash flow was a daily problem to be reckoned with at Spotland. The ebullient chairman of Rochdale A.F.C. was the 'larger than life' personality of Freddie Ratcliffe. Freddie was the 'king of the spring makers' and founded his own company in 1942. He had started his career at Riley's Spring Works where he took a seat on the board in 1939 at the tender age of 25. This was a pivotal year for Ratcliffe not only in his elevation to the dizzying heights of company directorship but the breaking out of WWII. His company thrived throughout the war years, as did many in the home based engineering business, and his personal wealth enabled him to take what many regarded as a near 'all consuming' interest in forwarding the ambitions of Rochdale Football Club. However, even the pockets of Freddie Ratcliffe were not bottomless.

It was said that anyone wishing to describe a typical dilapidated football ground of 1960s northern England, would do little better than look in the direction of Spotland. Len Hilton, a director of the club at the start of the 60s commented … 'We had holes in the ceiling and the whole place was like a shanty town. We simply had little or no money to improve things, but everyone who came to matches seemed to enjoy it!'

On a Friday, when it was time to pay the bills, Tony Collins recalls that everyone had to make a compromise somewhere and one or two creditors would not be paid. If anyone rang to complain to the club secretary, they would be told … 'well things are very tight right now, so each week we put everybody into the hat and make a draw … and if you don't stop complaining, you won't even go into the hat!' So there you have it. In the days before sponsorship and TV rights payments, a football club had to pay its way from gate money and the sale of pies on the terraces. It was a tough business and managing it required tough decision makers. So was Tony Collins up to the mark?

Appointing Tony as player-manager however was a popular move with the players and an economically satisfying decision by the chairman. It was up to Tony now to prove he could lead and improve a team under the assertion by Freddie Ratcliffe that … 'A town needs a football club in the Football League and that's always been the case for me!'

In a local newspaper article, comment was made about the appointment referring to Tony as spending the previous 12 years travelling some of the 'less fashionable' spots of English football. It noted that the quiet 34 year old was, in the words of the chairman, "A coloured boy!" He went on to explain the job was offered from a list of around 30 applicants and Tony Collins was the best, so for Ratcliffe, the choice was a simple one. He did underline what he may have considered to be one reasonable concern however with the following quote:

'We were aware that eyebrows might be raised because of his colour. But that made no difference, and we sincerely hope that it will make no difference in his career as manager'

The players were all behind him; his pedigree as a player was hard to beat and he knew the game and many of the big names in it through his experiences in the south. Best of all ... he could now spread his wings and test all of his theories regarding what he knew to be the science of the game.

So, the new philosophy of the completely new management was to encourage rather than chastise and bring out the very best in each player. The fear of making mistakes was slowly replaced by confidence in an individual's own playing ability. Tony demonstrated to his team as a player himself, a fearless approach to defenders, taking them on with foot skills rather than brute force and ignorance. He was also a frustrated tactician and he wanted, in fact needed, to be able to prove several theories of play he had studied as part of his playing career. The various methods of attack and defence related to a player's positioning on the pitch and although they often had odd names attached to them such as the 'Danubian School', 'Metodo' and the 'Magic Rectangle', such playing formations came mainly out of Europe and Brazil. The actual formations were titled by numbers such as 4-2-4, 4-2-2-2, and 3-3-1-3. The numbering system was developed in the middle to late 1950s and Tony Collins was an unashamed student of the tactics involved and the advantages of positioned play that could be transferred to the pitch.

As Player-Manager at Rochdale, he was not able to effectively cultivate what were at the time considered by most followers of the game in the North West to be revolutionary tactics. To most, the game of football, although listed as a non-contact sport, was in reality anything less. Full backs were normally tasked with stopping the opposing player with the ball … in whatever way necessary and forwards relied upon sheer speed to simply avoid them. This kind of philosophy would often provide what was termed by fans at the time as 'unattractive football' with both sides playing a defensive game and hell bent on stopping the ball getting into the back of their own net.

However, the chance to employ some fairly new tactics and philosophies as a team manager would come along sooner than expected when Tony received a bad knee injury forcing him off the pitch for over seven months. During this time, the team at Rochdale suffered some poor results; poor enough for Tony to forsake his regular treatment visits to Salford Hospital and get in shape for the local 'Derby' game against a determined Stockport County. Some local unidentified newspapers let everyone know what was going on, making a final comment:

'Tony, one of Soccer's top tacticians, played his last game against Oldham in the final match of last season. But recent sad displays by the Rochdale team have prompted him to hurry his return.'

Unfortunately, all did not go Rochdale's way against Stockport and it was at this point Tony knew that things would have to change. Whatever Tony's situation was off the field, on it he was a target for the heavy bruisers in defence … and he knew it. What would keep him fit, healthy and out of hospital would be skill and speed and of course, as Tony became older, so it would become more and more difficult to maintain a level of fitness necessary to keep him out of trouble with players some ten years his junior. At over 30 years of age, most football players of the day would be looking hard for another less physically demanding career. But for Tony, as a player, the accolades still kept coming and as a manager, many were taking a close look at his tactical work with one of the most underfunded teams in the English League.

Ratcliffe and his team in the board room were doing their best and as much as it is unrealistic to expect nowadays, teams that took to the field on a regular basis relied simply on gate money to pay all the wages and bills as well as player transfer fees. Rochdale unfortunately had one of the worst attendance figures in the league and no matter what kind of 'beautiful game' was played at Spotland, the numbers of individuals enthused enough to come week after week to watch the team were dismally low.

So, with Tony Collins acting as Player-Manager, nursing a knee that was simply not capable of supporting continuous fast and furious moves on the pitch, everyone at Rochdale knew their now less effective winger would have to settle into the job of full time manager in the hope that this tactical genius could start the process of nailing some trophies to the wall. With his contract running until the end of the 1961-62 season, a new three year contract as full time manager was put in front of Tony on September 5th, 1961. The annual salary on offer to the cash strapped club was £1,250.0.0 per annum (approx £26,000.00 at today's value) paid weekly, plus expenses … and so the new 'boss' at Spotland knew he had a challenge on his hands. Just to provide some sort of comparison as to what could be purchased at the time, in the equivalent of today's sterling value, a Mini car would have set someone back £496.00, petrol was 5p a litre, an FA Cup Final Ticket cost £2.50, a portion of Fish and Chips 6p and 20 Cigarettes 20p.

Being the part of the country that it was, no one could expect to hold a high profile position locally and not be labelled by the press. In Tony's case it was 'Teacher!' and the new title featured in this headline and article from an unidentified newspaper of the day, reviewing his performance some months into his job as manager.

Teacher Tony's idea is working out — *'Time was when blackboards were confined to the classroom at Rochdale. Now they are an important part of Spotland's football furniture. "Keep trying lads" used to be Rochdale's only pre-match plan … But that was before "teacher" Tony Collins came to town.'*

There were mixed views about Collins's 4-2-4 plan that had been the basis of Rochdale's soccer play. But it caused a lot of argument amongst the pundits, with the main comment being Rochdale did not have the players of the individual ability to master this revolutionary new method.

Unlucky — Oh, no? — *'The grumblers should have been at Oakwell last Saturday when the Spotland side were knocked out of the Cup in such an unlucky fashion. Whatever manager Collins's feelings about his club's Cup exit he must have been more than satisfied with the way his 4-2-4 plan worked.'*

The article also raised the subject that Rochdale seemed to have lost their finishing power. However, it was noticed by many that the new playing methods would not necessarily take the excitement out of the game, making it more like chess than football …

'But don't think Mr Collins is sacrificing fire for fancy football. He is determined to have both … and when he does Rochdale will start going places.'

Theory being put into practice was now the 'name of the game' and

Tony was convinced this was the way to go. So what was the real problem at Rochdale? Well everyone knew that a side playing good or bad football could not ever rise through the League tables without having money to buy players. The fact of the matter was that the local sports commentators thought quite openly the town of Rochdale did not deserve their team and one unidentified individual commented:

> Do Rochdale public deserve success? – *'An average home attendance of 3,500 from a population of 90,000 (bigger than Burnley's) suggests not.'*

The Chairman of Rochdale A.F.C. echoed the feeling in a public comment he made in the same article.

> Chairman Fred Ratcliffe said recently: – *'If it were not for our supporters club and our pool we should not be able to exist on our gates. We should lose hundreds of pounds a week. We would need gates of 6,000 or 7,000.'*

So, it appeared that bringing in Tony Collins, a possibly polished and more studious manager than most, would be seen as attempting to bring success and good football to a town that didn't seem to care!

With the new mantle of manager came all the necessary frustration of attempting to build a league winning team with no money to spend. That not only meant no money for new players but no money for any kind of extras or expenses for players already on the team. A small illustration of what could be the difference between a player giving his all on the pitch every time he stepped on it ... or having at the back of his mind the constant worry about how he was to get home from the match is worth noting. Joe Richardson was a young keen player for Rochdale but he lived some miles away from Spotland and had to catch a bus to and from the ground. Bus fares therefore became a big item in his weekly budget, but if he wanted to play football, then he would have to pay the bus fares as well. Tony picked up on the problem and after some possibly heated discussion with the club accountants he had the Richardson lad's bus fare paid as part of his wages. From that day on, this young eager player gave his all for his team and his manager, as this one simple act solved all of his financial issues and allowed him to do what he was there for ... play football!

So has it always been the case that only money can build a winning side, as still appears to be the situation in the 21st Century with teams like Manchester United and Chelsea etc? Well, it certainly looks like it with successful sides in the higher divisions either having fantastic gates or wealthy, altruistic Chairmen with deep, well padded pockets. Journalist Paul Doherty summed up the situation at Spotland when Tony Moulden left for Peterborough United.

Moulden decision was tough for Dale – *'Rochdale's team building twosome – manager Tony Collins and chief scout Jimmy Porter – were faced with their toughest heartbreak decision for many months at Spotland this week.'*

He went on to describe the rather bold offer by Peterborough United of £5,000 for Tony Moulden and the eagerness of the Rochdale board to accept it. It would be natural, said the Rochdale directors, not to be able to refuse such a sum for someone the manager had brought to the club only some five months previously at no cost whatsoever. Paul Doherty also noted that some credit must be allocated to Collins and Porter when around £7,000 had been collected by the club so far in exchange for players who had generally cost the club nothing. However, with such regular movements of players it was going to be difficult for Tony to build a team at Rochdale and he wanted it to be known.

But all was not lost at Spotland as Tony persevered with his new playing methodology and getting the most out of his players by encouragement and quality training techniques. The resulting headlines were not therefore cruel, as one would expect, but encouraging to a manager who was putting his heart and soul into the job. Below is an example headline from an unidentified newspaper of the day possibly written by Paul Doherty.

Half term wonders? – Not Dale – *'Everything in the Rochdale garden is lovely … except for those so grim gates'*

The reporter described the situation aptly in that despite Rochdale looking at promotion and achieving success in the League Cup, good gates were still hard to come by. It was surely true that their local football team were considered poor odds amongst the betting fraternity, but Rochdale had a good core of players despite two being sold for that desperately needed cash, both of whom were considered to be part of the planned-for winning formulae.

It was true that under Tony's guidance, Rochdale had arrived at the final of the 1962 League Cup where they lost 4–0 on aggregate in a two legged final to Norwich City, the first time a bottom league division club had reached the final of a major competition … and now they were chasing promotion. Local unaccredited press comment was as follows:

Top Show – *'Rochdale manager Tony Collins did well to look delighted after his team's fine win at Oldham. Nor was his enthusiasm about his inside forwards George Morton and Joe Richardson unreasonable. Morton is only 19 and Richardson only 20.'*

The article confirmed they scored two goals apiece and how well they – and the whole team – played the match. It also noted that Collins had made a shrewd move when he took 19 year-old outside left David Storf from Sheffield Wednesday for absolutely nothing.

But such general praise relating to Rochdale's performance was not to last for the whole of the 1962–63 season. This was naturally lamented by the local press who were very much on Rochdale's side in terms of where their game needed to go and the need to attack the apathy of local sports fans who persistently refused to turn up at home matches and support their own team. Further unaccredited press comment continued:

Why, oh why, this collapse late in season? – *'Tuesday night's win against Lincoln City was Rochdale's second in nine games from which they have collected seven points and scored five goals.'*

There was concern however that if the trend remained to the very last match it would be in keeping with the falling-off usually witnessed in the concluding stages of a season at Spotland. There seemed to be no sound reason why a team which can average more than a point a game for most of the campaign is not able to do so in the last quarter of the season.

Tony Collins commented, stating that a falling away in performance towards the end of the season had much to do with the size and strength of the squad being carried. When choice is strictly limited, first team players are effectively overworked. With a small squad to pick from, when players were injured there were no 'fresh legs' to take their place. The unknown reporter noted:

'There could well be truth in this for in recent weeks Rochdale's trouble has been in the attack and the forward selection has had to be made from only seven professionals. Experiments with defenders could be tried, of course, but they are gambles and often don't come off.'

After being runners up in the League Cup, it was expected that due to all the publicity and enthusiasm surrounding such a great effort fans would be prompted to get behind their team and turn up for matches. But that was unfortunately not the case as confirmed by the following unaccredited comment in the local press.

Sore point – *'Gates are a sore point with me'* said Rochdale's professor of Soccer know-how, manager Tony Collins. *'I don't like to talk about attendances, but we should not fare too badly on Saturday.'*

In the run up to the League Cup final in the previous season, Rochdale received much attention in the local and National press being the lowest division level team ever to have got there. The following match report is from an unidentified newspaper of the day.

Rochdale Ride Out Storm – *Fourth Division Rochdale survived the siege at Ewood Park last night to reach the final of the Football League Cup. It took Blackburn only eight minutes to pull back one goal from the 3-1 lead that Rochdale held from the first leg of the semi-final. And it took no longer for Rochdale's tactics to be revealed. They adopted a system of retreating defence that even the Austrian team would have admired. From the moment that Fred Pickering scored from a penalty after Bryan Douglas had been fouled, Rochdale sounded "the retreat" on Ewood's muddy battlefield. Seven players, including centre forward Louis Bimpson, locked, barred and bolted Blackburn's path to goal. The stage was so fierce, the exchanges so tough that tin hats, full packs and rifles might have been more in keeping with the situation than football kit. The tactics paid off handsomely. As a result of this win Rochdale collect £20-a-man and write their own chapter in the League Cup's brief history.'*

After the bloody battle with local rivals Blackburn, the final played over two legs did unfortunately fail to go Rochdale's way. Norwich played well to beat Rochdale 4–0 on aggregate with a 3–0 result at Spotland and a 1–0 win at Carrow Road. The disappointment was obvious but the pride of simply getting into the final was a suitable return for all the effort the team had put in. No one knew better than Tony Collins how difficult it had been to clamber into the League Cup final with Norwich City, having little choice of fit players, no money to purchase fresh players and no gate money to refresh the crumbling facilities at the Spotland facility. But in the world of professional football, things were changing – for better or worse!

~~~~

In 1957, Jimmy Hill had become Chairman of the Professional Footballer's Association (PFA), an institution that was in effect the player's union. Once in this influential position he campaigned tirelessly to have the £20 maximum wage for players as defined by the Football League, changed and eventually scrapped. This was a substantial achievement in 1961 especially considering the ongoing litigation between George Eastham and Newcastle United concerning a refused transfer request. The PFA, under the guidance of Hill, financed Eastham's legal battle with the beleaguered top flight club which was to be relegated to the Second Division for the 1961–62 season. The Judge finally made a decision in 1963 with unfavourable comment regarding the 'Retain and Transfer' system of controlling just about every element of a football player's life.

As a result of actions taken by the PFA, the high court ruled that the 'Retain and Transfer' system was unjustifiable; a system that had been in effect since the early 1890s. It is not necessary to investigate the details of the system here, but suffice to say the benefit lay more or less with the club and its ownership and not with the player. At that time, not one club in the country wanted to change the *status quo*, as limiting the wages of players and taking literally all of any transfer money paid for a player, enhanced the club's finances and enabled a board of directors to view the management mantra to be profit rather than the promotion of the game. No-one expected all club chairmen to be fully paid up philanthropists, but neither did players or fans expect their local club to be so profit oriented as to negatively affect team quality.

So, the period 1961 to 1963 was a time of change in the world of professional football. To watch a full game at that time required a visit to the stadium where the match was being played. The quickly improving television service, offered exclusively by the BBC, covered some matches on its Saturday night 'Sports Special' programme which aired brief highlights of matches in a service that lasted from 1955 to 1963. But standing in the wings was a new commercial television channel named ITV who knew that the way to 'take on' the BBC, as part of its quest for audience figures in order to satisfy its advertisers, was to televise football matches. Again, under an agreement with Jimmy Hill's PFA, a deal was made for the 1960-61 season between the Football League and the ITV worth £150,000 agreeing the rights to a live broadcast of 26 matches. Compared to today's deals of billions of pounds, this does not appear to be a lot of money, but at an equivalent value in 2015, this amounts to over £3.1 million.

This attempt to get behind the popularity of 'the beautiful game' unfortunately fell at the first hurdle with some top line clubs refusing permission to provide coverage from their grounds, along with the Football League putting forward a demand for a substantial increase in player appearance money. Another attempt was made in 1962 when Anglia Television launched a new show named 'Match of the Week', but the big impetus, propelling the game to the kind of coverage it receives today was to be the World Cup tournament being held in England in 1966. Today, as a direct result of that tournament, the live coverage it received and the interest it created, English Premier League matches are broadcast to more than 600 million people in over 200 countries worldwide.

CHAPTER SEVEN

The Trials and Tribulations of Management!

T he middle 60s would change the face of professional football for ever. Jimmy Hill's teammate at Fulham and England Captain, Johnny Haynes, is reputed to be the very first player to earn £100 per week as official wages in 1961 … and there would be many more to come despite efforts by clubs such as Liverpool and Manchester United to enforce a maximum wage of £50 per week.

With TV companies and the BBC now airing regular programmes relating specifically to football, Tony became a regular interviewee, earning a steady four guineas a time (£4.4s.0d) for his contributions. Unfortunately, Rochdale's progress after defeat in the League Cup was not necessarily 'onward and upward' from that point but had rather 'see-sawed' through the fourth division of the Football League at 7th in the 62–63 season, 20th in the 63–64 season, 6th in the 64–65 season and 21st in the 65–66 and 66–67 seasons … requiring the club to be re-elected to the League on both occasions.

The *Manchester Evening News* commented about that particular time in the club's history stating that the mid 60s had become a real battle for survival as a professional football club. It revealed details of the trip

Fred Ratcliffe made to Football league Headquarters in Soho Square, London in an attempt to have the club re-elected to the league. As previously described, the bottom four clubs were required to perform this ritual annually, with one inevitably being dropped. However, Fred was a great personality who could win friends when it mattered and it mattered to keep Rochdale in the game of football. He was passionate about the game as well as his town and succeeded twice with the FA when it really was needed.

With all requests for funding of new players falling on deaf ears, Tony Collins as manager was taking much flak from the press and fans alike. It was an uncomfortable position to be in although there was some good news on the personal front when on the 24th of July, 1964 Edith gave birth to a daughter, Sarita Diane. It was a very happy time for both Edith and Tony and they were well settled in their house at Edenfield Road.

To make that time absolutely perfect, all Tony needed was to have been given some money to buy one or two players because he knew that in the 64–65 season, Rochdale could have moved into a promotion position. The board knew of Tony's frustrations, but they also knew of their responsibilities to somehow keep the club afloat financially. Unfortunately, communications had started to breakdown and rumours had begun to grow to such an extent that a local press interview with the vice-chairman of the club offered to the public a view of their feelings regarding their beleaguered manager. Many who knew the real reason for lack of progress at Rochdale would regard some of the comments made by a member of the board and vice-chairman, Mr Tattersall as rather 'tongue in cheek'! This headline, possibly from the *Manchester Evening News* and with an article probably written by Eric Thornton, tells the story.

Rochdale Wouldn't Swop Boss Collins – *'Rochdale, one of the Fourth Division humbler outfits when it comes to totting up the turnstile figures, showed in their own modest way in midweek that success cannot be bought.'*

Thornton tells how the 'Dale' smashed Doncaster Rovers 3-1, a team that had spent over £30,000 that season on players, despite having injuries of their own to contend with. The vice-chairman at Rochdale was interviewed confirming that if there was a transfer market in managers, then they would have been one of the richest teams in the area. He also made a comforting statement by saying that 'Now we would not swap Tony Collins for anybody!' Tony himself made comment stating very clearly that 'We could all use more support. Who could not? But unfortunately a club without the history of a first division spell behind it at one time or another seems to breed a very pessimistic brand of supporter, and even a winning run does not seem to bump up the gate a lot. Our big task now is to try and hold on to the promising material we have until it finally registers in the eyes of the Rochdale public that we have a team which is improving all the time, and is worth watching'. To back up this claim, Tony confirmed he was very proud of his second team composed mainly of teenagers who had won 10 matches in a row in the Lancashire League.

There was often some unexpectedly generous support for Tony in the local and National press, eager to tell the story of 'The Miracle' as most would call it in managing a team on what other managers would consider to be a 'shoestring' budget. Eric Thornton, on behalf of the *Manchester Evening News* in his 'Outposts of Soccer' series, would produce a rather hard-hitting article in 1965 exploring what was happening at Spotland and accompanied by a rather sensational headline.

Miracle Man Has Spent Only £15,000 In Five Years – *'Tony Collins belongs to a brotherhood in which many shout their wares and bawl about their performances, and echoes come back with a hollowness.'*

However, Thornton goes on to clarify this rather confusing declaration by stating that in his view, although few really stand out from the others, one certainly does and he is the young Rochdale manager Tony Collins who he claims performs a near miracle by managing a professional football club on a literal pennies and pounds budget. He says that Rochdale is one of Britain's poorest clubs, has one of the smallest crowds and one of the smallest wage bills. He noted that if his team could attract the kind of crowd attendances that wealthy clubs enjoyed, then Collins could 'spread his wings' and challenge the other clubs in higher divisions for a fair share of the silverware. The job of Collins was in effect to plan putting a team on the field each week that needed to win with no money to spare in the bank, have to work out some quite cunning plans to capture free-transfer players and at the same time make sure that travelling expenses are minimal. Thornton gave Collins credit for always fielding a fit, capable and fighting football team and spending no more than £15,000 since he took over the reins at Rochdale some five years previously. He quotes Tony as saying:

'It must be nice to go after every player you fancy, knowing you've a pretty good chance of landing some of them, but there is plenty of interest in life even when there is not the money to spend. In fact, the lack of it keeps you even more wide awake than ever because of the absolute necessity of everlastingly watching and keeping your eyes skinned for the slightest chance of picking up a useful buy at give-away prices or even less. Of course many others are in the same game, all wanting to get bargains, just like women on shopping expeditions.

With poorer clubs, of course, it is usually a case of trying to pick up experienced players for next-to-nothing and hoping to get a few more years of good service out of them, or finding the youngster of promise who has not just hit it off with one club'

The article also revealed that Collins took on the job as manager at Rochdale as the result of a boardroom vote in competition with 30 others. Perhaps when the club failed to achieve promotion after two strong attempts, a flicker in the so far strong and determined flame of ambition started to appear and as such Tony made even more vehement representations to the board to fund the movement of players. There was obviously speculation amongst the fans and the local press about the situation of the manager at Rochdale.

The board at Rochdale had signed a new contract with Collins in February 1963, extending his contract for a further five years at a salary of £1,500.0.0 per annum, a monetary increase of £250.0.0 a year and a percentage increase of 20%. Would that be a big enough financial incentive to hold Tony Collins down and keep him in his job at Spotland? There were those in the March of 1965 who did not think so and some voiced their opinion quite openly. The following three report headlines are from an unknown source but probably originated with *The Manchester Evening News.*

No Comment on Oldham Speculation – *'Is Mr Tony Collins to move from Spotland to Boundary Park to manage Oldham Athletic?'*

The article went on to speculate that the Rochdale manager could well be moving on to nearby Oldham Athletic. It reported the Collins' preference to provide a 'No Comment!' answer to all questioning which did nothing to quell curiosity. The reporter did remind his readers of the successes of Tony and his team taking Rochdale to the Football League Cup final. It particularly highlighted the transfer deal involving Tony Moulden and the performance of Reg Jenkins with comment relating to Tony's remarkable ability to spot a player and move him to the club at a minimal transfer fee, or none at all.

Reporter John Kay wrote a quite revealing article in an unnamed newspaper at the time confirming that Collins, in his third season at Spotland as manager could look back with some pride at what had been achieved. He quoted Freddie Ratcliffe who said:

'We do not want to lose him. He has a completely free hand and is living up to the high standard set by Catterick and Marshall.'

Kay reported Tony's denial of any planned move from Rochdale adding that he was happy at Spotland but would of course consider any chance to better himself. He admitted that most of the existing side at Rochdale had been bought at what could only be regarded as bargain prices. An example of such a transaction was once again quoted as that of Tony Moulden on a free transfer from Bury and selling him on to Peterborough for over £60,000. It went on to list names of players such as Ted Burgin, Doug Winton, Jimmy Thompson, Doug Wragg, Don Watson, Peter Phoenix and George Morton; all of whom had been on the Collins list of good transfer deals. Kay stated that despite the exit of Whittaker and Moulden, the team at Rochdale were still in good shape for promotion. Finally, Kay's conclusion was that although handicapped in most areas, Collins had done a good job so far and that would be why another club with more money to spend and attracting bigger crowds would find this particular manager just what they could be looking for.

In June 1964 a new kid on the block arrived at Spotland in the shape of inside forward Reg Jenkins. He was signed for £2,250 from Torquay and it is said that with the guidance of Tony Collins he had found his true footballing home ... and that was probably not too far from the truth. He scored two goals in his first match for Rochdale. The headlines giving out the news of the signing in a local newspaper were more a sign of relief than the trumpeting of a major coup by Collins.

'Big Inside-Forward At Last'

The fee was not a record for the club but was in fact pretty close to it. Jenkins was a Cornishman born at Millbrook near Plymouth and had spent his playing career in the West Country. Up to the point of signing, Reg admitted he didn't know where Rochdale was let alone Spotland and there were concerns that he might not settle well into northern culture. However he stayed at Rochdale happily until 1974 making 305 appearances and scoring 119 goals ... a club record. It turned out to be a good week for Collins who, after signing Jenkins homed in on a Bolton reserves wing-half named James Graham Cunliffe who was signed on a free transfer.

However, like it or not, times change and the Spotland residents were now languishing at the bottom of the Third Division and only just missing relegation. Tony did in effect feel secure in his contract which had three years to run and there was no doubt he was a young and successful manager. The board had placed their confidence in him when they extended his contract to five years.

Shrewd Buying — *'In the season just finished Collins, by shrewd buying on a limited budget, hoisted his team into a challenging promotion position, and they narrowly missed going into Division Three. His achievements have not gone unnoticed by Oldham and you can watch for developments soon.'*

The whole situation of press speculation and rumour surrounding a possible move from Spotland was unsettling for Tony Collins, who at this particular time was regularly beating down the door of his chairman, begging for more funds to build the Rochdale team. However, before the story of the sacking of the Oldham manager was voiced so publicly in March, the rumour mill was in full production and Tony rang Les McDowell, whilst he was still the Oldham manager, to tell him quite firmly there was no truth in any speculation that the Oldham chairman had been talking to him and that whatever public frustrations were actually voiced, he was committed to Rochdale. It has to be understood that at that particular time, there were only 92 manager's jobs in the whole professional football arena and most club boards would have someone in mind to replace any manager before they sacked him. Sometimes the approaches would be direct, consisting of a simple phone call and other approaches could be more subtle, such as slipping out a story to the press in the expectation that the manager named would contact the club chairman and open up a conversation.

However, all of the speculation at Oldham led eventually to local lad Gordon Hurst taking up the weighty mantle, lasting only one season and leaving Tony undisturbed in his efforts to improve the Rochdale side … against all the odds. The strange thing was that in the July of 1967, Hurst would play another off-stage part in shaping the events in Tony's life once again when he was taken on at Spotland as the new trainer-coach.

Tony was well respected by many managers and players across the Football league system and Stan Cullis, who had taken over the reins at

Second Division Birmingham City in the December of 1965, was looking for some form of co-operation. Stan was a strong, well respected manager who had guided Wolverhampton Wanderers to a firm place near the top of the Second Division from 1948 to 1964. A statue to him stands to this day outside the Wolves Molineux Stadium and when he was surprisingly sacked in September 1964, he vowed never to work in football again. However, he was eventually tempted to join Birmingham City and after taking up the post unfortunately failed to repeat the success he had created at Wolves.

He wrote to Tony on October 7th, 1966 and the contents of his letter confirm the kind of reputation the Rochdale manager had at that time amongst other managers.

> *'Dear Tony,*
>
> *I was hoping to be able to see you at a match, possibly in mid week, to have a chat to you on the question of mutually assisting each other. I can probably give you some help and what I would like you to do is to let me know of any promising youngsters you may see on your travels.*
>
> *The reason I write to you is that I value your opinion and your straight way of dealing. I make a rule to keep in touch with managers who I respect to be of mutual assistance to each other.*
>
> *Yours sincerely,*
>
> *S. Cullis.'*

By ending up at 21st in the Division for both the 65–66 and 66–67 seasons, Rochdale was forced to seek re-election twice. The club was in trouble and the frustrations for Tony Collins were piling up. He wanted to get on in life; he now had three children to look after … and was not getting any younger. Eventually, the inevitable headline generated by one well informed Geoff Whitworth with a column in an unidentified newspaper of the day, but probably *The Manchester Evening News*, eventually appeared:

Players Will Petition Board: – *'Keep Collins – When the Rochdale chairman, Mr F S Ratcliffe, arrives at Spotland this afternoon he will receive a petition from some of the players which will ask the board to reinstate Mr Tony Collins as manager "if at all possible.'*

The report was correct and a petition had been drawn up after Tony had called all the players together and told them he was no longer to be their manager. He stated the reason to be a matter of principle and confirmed that Gordon Hurst who had recently joined the club as a Trainer-Coach would act as Caretaker-Manager until someone else could be found to take over the hot seat. The Chairman issued a statement:

'I am sorry that that the position is such that Tony is leaving us. After being present in London when he was signed by the club as a player, and later being responsible for his promotion to player-manager, I have a lot of regrets that he has found it necessary to resign. As a man, we are going to have a struggle to find a better manager than Tony. Running a football club is not just putting 11 players out on the field. The business acumen that Tony has is above average and in this respect any negotiations he has carried out were carried out with one thought in mind, the benefit of the club, either by bringing players in to the advantage of the club or by selling players, equally to the advantage of the club. Team building took second place to managing the club and the financial position was ever present in his mind. I hope he is successful in getting a job which will prove my views regarding his ability. In fact I feel confident that his knowledge of football will probably get him a plum job in the game. With regard to the future, team selection and discipline will be in the

hands of Gordon Hurst and he has the full backing of the board in this capacity. This was made perfectly clear at the last board meeting. The position will now be advertised and we hope to appoint a successor as soon as possible.

I feel we have a stronger side this season as a result of the new players signed in the close season and I look forward to the spectators giving the team and directors encouragement. I hope there will be no 'knocking' from the handful who are always looking for faults and lashing people with their tongues. Finally, I want it to be known that I have personally invited Tony Collins to come to Rochdale and watch the matches from the directors' box any time he pleases. This has been done because I have a great admiration for him and would hate to think of him as just another manager going away from his first love.'

Tony of course had to issue some form of statement although he was reluctant to do so. He did not wish to answer questions about his reasons of principle because he felt that his discussions with the board were confidential and pushed as he was to give out more details, he refused to do so. His statement was short and to the point:

'I have resigned and the board is prepared to pay my contract up in full to the end of the season. It has been a question of principle. I think the team will do well this season because there has not been one game in which we were at full strength. There is always someone out. Once there is a full complement, and providing the crowd gives them a chance, they will do well. You have a wonderful camp here!'

When pushed many times at the news conference to explain the reasons for his resignation further, Tony's reply was:

'I have nothing further to add!'

News about the petition was presented by the team captain, Brian

Taylor who wanted to make it clear the team were not in revolt confirmed they would do their very best for whoever finally took charge at Spotland. However, they wanted their views known and felt that a petition was the right way of going about it. So, good bad or indifferent, the news was finally out, the decision made and there would be no going back. Tony Collins was leaving Rochdale. The real situation was of course a little more complicated than simply being a 'point of principle', and Tony explains the reason for leaving as follows.

In the 1964–65 season the team were running for promotion. Collins knew that he desperately needed one or two players to strengthen the team in case of injuries, which were a constant problem. He put two players up to the board who were flying high on the recent good run of the team in the division and as far as they were concerned, they could be in a promotion position without having to spend money on any more players. However, they just missed out and with an exhausted, over-played team with no real quality reserves, the standards of play started to drop and there was little that Tony could do about it.

From a commercial point of view, the board were very happy at some spectacularly successful commercial results Tony had engineered during his previous three years as full time manager and felt that the money they now had would be better spent on the fabric of the club rather than the team. Unless Tony could repeat such successes by only spotting talent on free transfer, then there was to be no new blood for the team any time soon. David Cross had been sold to Norwich City for £40,000 and Alan Taylor moved on to West Ham for a similar figure. There had been the sale of Tony Moulden to Peterborough and Colin Whitaker to Oldham; two movements that literally destroyed a long term team building plan in the mind of Tony Collins. The acquisition from Sheffield Wednesday of a young 19 year old outside left, David Storf for nothing was also the kind of coup that the board thought Collins could repeat time and time again – but they were of course quite wrong.

The situation with the missed signing of George Graham is a typical example of what Tony was up against at the time and he recalls the situation in his own words as follows.

'They called George Graham 'Stroller' when he was a player and it wasn't a bad nickname. There was a kind of strolling elegance, almost arrogance about Graham when he played the game. He had real style and a load of ability, and it was obvious even when he was a kid. Nowadays, years later, there might not seem much connection between a struggling Northern club like Rochdale and George Graham, one time boss at Arsenal, Leeds and Spurs. But when I was manager at Rochdale, my old chief scout Jimmy Porter rang me up one day with a tip. Porter was a great value; he used to put me wise on a lot of things about the game in my early management years.

"Today, I've got a bargain for you," said Jimmy. I pulled the phone a bit closer and listened. You know when Porter recommended someone, he was worth hearing about. "There's a lad in Aston Villa's reserves named George Graham who is going to make a great player one day. He's yours if you can raise six grand because the boy is desperate to get away and play first team football anywhere."

Six grand may not sound much these days, but the most I ever spent as Rochdale manager was £2,600, so this needed thinking about. I went to my board of directors and told them what was on my mind. "I'm only bringing this up because I don't want anyone to come back later and say didn't we know about him," I told them. "I know we can't afford this but there's a lad in Villa's reserves who's going to be some player. Trouble is he will cost us £6,000."

Freddie Ratcliffe, my Chairman at the time, surprisingly asked me for more details. I told him Graham was 18, but I knew that the club would have a good player for ten years. Or, if he moved on, they'd make a lot of money out of a future transfer. "In that case," said Ratcliffe, "I would like to go for him." I should think that the look on my face was interesting, to say the least.

Alas, the dream did not last long. The other members of the board promptly set about talking Ratcliffe out of it. They said bluntly "We cannot afford it!"

A few days later, Tommy Docherty, the manager at Chelsea, moved in and signed George Graham for £8,000. What a snip! I found that so frustrating working for clubs in the lower leagues. Many a time I saw a player and thought to myself "Blimey, he would do for us" But it is very hard to accept when you see talent but you cannot get it.'

With the doors firmly shut to any further real finance, the team's performance dropped significantly with injuries taking a severe toll and over-playing of certain team stalwarts proving unsustainable. For the last full season of Tony's tenure, the club had to be re-elected to the league and naturally, the manager was getting 'some stick' from the fans – few as they seemed to be! During this difficult time, the board remained completely silent and Tony felt he was perhaps being left as the scapegoat in a process of general, slow decline. The decision to leave Spotland was a difficult one for Tony and not taken lightly, but the situation the club was left in by the October of 1967 was untenable. Rochdale were heading for the bottom Division spot once again and to Tony, it looked as if re-election would, once more, be their only saviour.

However, communications between the board and Tony remained good and on October 23rd, 1967 the club agreed a compensation payment to their resigned manager of £1,250. There would be much discussion after the event amongst fans and board members. Rochdale had taken the Collins family to their heart and Edith was very settled there. The house in Edenfield Road had become the physical anchor for them all and Edith had put much love into the bricks and mortar, placing her stamp on what was now their home. There would be no more moving house if she had anything to do with it, and although she was well aware that being a football player or manager was a transitory business, there had to come a point where family and stability took centre stage in the planning of Tony's future career moves. So what would be next?

CHAPTER EIGHT

The Search Is On

Did Tony Collins have any specific ideas about what he would do with his life after leaving Rochdale A.F.C? Had he thought the whole process through … thoroughly? The club board had not wanted him to leave … and the players did not want him to leave, but in the autumn of 1967, Tony found himself at a crossroads and looking his 42nd birthday firmly in the face. However, his resignation was a 'matter of principle' and he felt comfortable with the decision and Edith backing him all the way. The children were growing rapidly with Sandra being a teenager at age 13, Andrew rapidly approaching his teenage years at 11 and young Sarita now a 3 year old handful. Perhaps the decision had finally been made that no matter what Tony did with his future career, he had now accepted his home would always be 54 Edenfield Road, Rochdale.

Like all men out of work, Tony did what he needed to do to pay the bills and provide security for his family. He had good contacts within what was now the rapidly growing industry of English Football and had earned respect from participants at all levels of the game. However, his ambition lay with management and he began the process of trying to find another club where he could be called 'boss' once more. Choice, by the nature of the job, was essentially limited but in the October of 1967 he wrote off to Watford, in November to Rotherham and Peterborough and in December to Macclesfield Town. In the first quarter of 1968 he made applications to Chester, Darlington and Stockport County ... all without success.

However, sitting on the sidelines, was Alan Dicks, the newly arrived Manager at Bristol City. He and Tony met at an Oldham match and Alan asked Tony to 'have a look' at his team the following week. After he gave out his 'no holds barred' report, Alan knew he had found what he was looking for ... an able assistant-manager. Bristol City was a Second Division club that had bounced between the Second and Third Divisions since the war, but it was also a club with ambition under the chairmanship of 71 year old Harry Dolman, and Alan Dicks wanted an assistant manager to join him on a real quest for promotion to the First Division. It didn't take long for Alan to convince Tony that joining Bristol was the right move for him and a salary of £2,000 a year, with some generous expenses attached, including the freedom to remain in his Rochdale home, was the 'clincher' as far as Tony and Edith were concerned. On December 1st, 1968, Tony Collins signed up for Bristol and a memorable partnership would start to take shape; one that would change the ambitions of the club enough to push them into the top two of the Second Division in the 75-76 season and eventually provide the longed for promotion to the top flight of English Football.

However, getting there was not going to be easy. The team had a good ground to play in at the 20,000 plus capacity Ashton Gate and received good local support with the nickname 'The Robins'. Alan Dicks took up his first position as manager from Coventry City where he had been assistant manager under Jimmy Hill. It was Jimmy who had recommended him and at an age of 33, with no real management experience behind him, it was a risk, but one the chairman of 'The Robins' was willing to take. The team had been languishing in a period of irregular and often poor performance and chairman Dolman wanted a more spirited concert from his team and was determined to get it.

Dicks knew he needed some support from someone with experience at a full managerial level and a person who could find players, and more importantly, buy players at the right price. Tony Collins therefore appeared to be just the man he needed and so a great working friendship was to be formed that would be reflected in a growing achievement for the team and positive results on the pitch. Unfortunately, Dolman was to be unseated as chairman in 1974 and replaced by a much younger Robert Hobbs who had made nearly all of his money in the quarrying business. However, Dolman's influence would remain as he took up the position of club President, a position he would hold until his death in 1977, and the Dolman legacy would not end there as the Presidency was passed on to Harry's wife, the young and vivacious Marina, who at the time of writing still takes up her place in the directors box at Ashton Gate, remaining one of Bristol City's most fervently loyal supporters. They had married in 1961 when Harry was 63 and she was just 24 with the event causing more than the expected level of general interest, having to 'dodge' reporters when leaving the wedding reception venue.

However much the Dolman fortunes had been used to support the club financially, a new chairman with a new bank balance and a new hunger for success was what was needed to push Bristol City back into the First Division, and the double act of Dicks and Collins were determined to get them there. This report by Mike Casey, probably from the *Bristol Post*, sums up the situation as he saw it.

Bristol City revival opens up the West! — *'If Bristol City can keep their nerve and their form for 11 more games the West Country next winter will have its first taste of First Division Soccer for 65 years.'*

He went on to remind City supporters that they were in fact First Division runners-up in the 1906-07 season, the year following their rise to the top of the Second Division. He quoted Collins as saying:

> *'The lads have worked particularly hard this season, and they're looking forward to sharing the limelight with the Liverpool's and Derby's. The trouble with a lot of teams is that they worry about how their rivals are faring"* he added. *"At Bristol we try to forget the others. Alan Dicks, the Manager, drills it into the lads that success or failure depends on their own efforts'*

Tony was confident after the previous years of preparation and careful buying policy that the club had what it would take to get into the First Division. Attendances, being a singularly important facet of club management, were rising to what the board regarded as a break-even level of 16,000 plus. This would mean that players did not have to be sold at the end of the season to finance day to day costs and expenses. The chairman, Hobbs also made statements relating to 'who was after who' in the transfer game and let out to all who were listening that the club had an overdraft of £200,000 and Ashton Gate as an operation, was losing close to £1,000 a week. Mike Casey made a further final comment reminding his readers that many clubs have financial problems and regardless of what might be said in public, every player has a price and if that price is substantial enough, then the temptation to collect the cash is sometimes overwhelming.

Of course, the situation with Collins as Assistant Manager living in Rochdale caught the eye of the National press finding that the club manager was living more or less 'on the job' and the assistant-manager residing some 200 miles away.

The unusual arrangement for Tony Collins was given some attention by the press although most agreed that Tony was travelling nearly 40,000 miles a year on his scouting activities and therefore it didn't really matter where he lived. Both Tony and Edith wanted to stay at Edenfield Road in Rochdale. It was home, and in the transient world of football management, it was also an anchor for the whole family. They had both planned it that way and wanted it to stay that way.

As an indication of what went on when Alan Dicks secured the services of Tony Collins on the basis of him staying at Rochdale, Tony comments:

> *'Then the idea of having an assistant manager based in the North didn't appeal to all the City board. They were worried about the cost factor and what I was doing with my time,' he said. 'But my job essentially is to go looking for players and Bristol could hardly be worse geographically. Where better to be situated than the North-West? There is one set of traffic lights between my house and Glasgow, London or Bristol. I can go anywhere in a few hours.'*

This of course was a sign of the times leaving one to wonder how today's motorway travellers in Britain would view such a remark. At that time Tony also made a few revealing comments relating to his tenure as boss at the Rochdale club.

> *'When I first joined Bristol, I had just finished at Rochdale. I became tired there of battling all the time, of having to send the electricity bill to the gas board and vice versa to buy time; of having to sell to survive. I'm not knocking Rochdale. I took them to the League Cup final in 1962 and that was a fairy-tale.'*

When talking further about his role at Bristol he said: – *It was a battle for the first few years. Alan and I used to sit up until three in the morning arguing about players. He had a rough time with everybody on his back. But the youngsters started to come through.'*

~~~~

The battles, of course, were related to money, and the movement of Harry Dolman from Club Chairman to a more honorary title of Club President appeared to be necessary to maintain an acceptable level of communication between the board and management.

Tony's bank manager was also pleased with the progress of Bristol City when in 1975 a three year contract was signed for a salary of £5,000 per annum with full expenses and a complex bonus structure. This basic salary would be worth some £38,000 at today's values and with all his expenses and car paid for, with a very healthy bonus scheme in place, this overall package would be considered a reasonable income by today's standards. As his reputation inside and outside the game continued to grow, Tony was called upon to give regular TV interviews and provide special articles for the sports sections of National newspapers.

As part of their team building programme, Dicks and Collins arranged for some matches involving foreign travel, such as the game between Iranian League champions Persepolis F.C. and City which took place in May 1972. The head coach in Tehran was an Englishman named Alan Rogers who encouraged the Iranian Football league winners from 1971 through 1976, to play with clubs outside the country in order to gain experience. The team was either owned or certainly well supported by the Shah of Iran, Mohammed Reza Pahlavi which allowed all the necessary paperwork to be completed permitting the match to actually take place. A local, but well known sports reporter inside Iran, Hushang Nemazee from the Iranian newspaper *Kayhan International*, gave this opinion of the encounter:

Bristol beat Persepolis – *'Bristol City turned in a vastly improved performance and clearly showed their mettle in beating Tehran club champions Persepolis 1-0 at Amjadieh Stadium yesterday afternoon. The English Second Division club scored almost at the start of the match and then kept their lead with gallant football which was in marked contrast to their performance in beating a weak Tehran XI 2-0 on Sunday.*

Bristol forward Spiring scored the match winner in the sixth minute. Tainton's kick was picked up by Jacobs whose shot was beautifully headed home by Spiring. The remainder of the match was full of action with both sides attacking and the ball repeatedly travelling up and down the field.'

The team arrived in Tehran with summer coming on at a pace. Tony described the climate as 'sweltering heat' and coming from a damp and slightly chilly Bristol with a team of young men rarely travelled outside of the UK, the climate, and in fact the whole event would be regarded as something of an eye-opener. Culture shock set in at the airport where the travellers were met with some weighty looking and heavy handed security. The Shah, someone completely consumed with security after being hospitalised due to a failed assassination attempt some years earlier, was living on borrowed time and foreigners were regarded with some suspicion – whoever they were. He therefore sent the head of his personal body guard to greet the visitors. This physically huge person with a deep, gruff voice who spoke little or no English, was named Raheem, and it was obvious he was there to give them the 'once over'! Simply getting on the bus was turned into a military operation with orders being barked out by the nervous security team. He carried a pistol with him at all times making some of the team visibly nervous. When Tony asked what the gun was for the Iranian replied: 'For protection, sport and – other things!'

Everyone arrived at a hotel in the centre of the city whose name was not specifically recorded but was probably the 4 star rated Hotel Sina, a favourite place for the government of the day to place foreigners. Air conditioning in 1972 was still quite a new innovation in Iran and both Tony and Alan Dicks knew the heat would become a problem. The team instructions were precise and clear: 'Relax as much as possible, keep as cool as possible and try not to expend too much energy!' The hosts however wanted to show everyone the town and keep their visitors busy so Tony and Alan had to lay down some ground rules. Players could go out and about after a match — but not before it. They had to avoid iced drinks for fear of stomach problems and be in the hotel and in bed by a certain time. There were some obvious moans and groans with comparisons made to much disliked 'school trips' but apart from that there was an air of excitement about the whole proceedings. The Shah sent one of his personal staff to look after the visitors, a guy named Ali Abdu, who was used to swaggering around his own people. He was a powerful and mostly feared gentleman with a direct connection to the Shah; someone who was regarded by many not simply as a ruler but a god. To beggars in the street Mr. Ali Abdu would throw coins in the air to simply see them scrambling in the dust and dirt and then be brought near to tears with gratitude for the 'kindness' of his act. Life was cheap in Tehran, as it was in many other parts of the Middle East at that time, with sadly not much changing now, and the players were surprised on the first night when a bundle of what looked like sheets possibly dropped on the corridor floor outside their room ... moved! They quickly discovered that between the sheets some of the cleaning staff could be found sleeping there. There was no other type of accommodation provided to such low level employees and they quickly assured their English visitors it was a perfectly normal situation to them.

Ali was an ignorant man and once when in the hotel he shouted over to the barman to get the 'kids' some drinks. Tony had to remind him: 'These men are professional football players – NOT kids!'

So, to the first game and on the morning of the match, Alan and Tony were told a tour of the city had been arranged which Alan scotched immediately. This did not go down well and the Iranian messenger advised Alan that the Shah himself had organised this 'gift' and would not be happy to see it refused.

'We'll do it tomorrow,' Tony advised the Iranian 'but not now – just before a game!'

The plan was obvious. The Iranians simply wanted to tire out the team before the match so the tour would have to be re-arranged for the next day. The messenger was petrified. There was no way he could tell the Shah that his kindness had been found unacceptable, but Alan quietly advised the young man that this was *'His problem!'* and *he* would have to sort it out.

The game was to be staged at the Amjadieh Stadium in Tehran and for some reason the driver had been instructed to take the 'scenic route' along the edge of the mountains on the north side of Tehran. The driver played Arabic and Farsi music continuously, clapping his hands in time with the drumming accompanied by Raheem and some of his cohorts, as he engineered the white knuckle ride along gravel roads with substantial drops to one side. The team was worried at the driver's lack of control, as was Tony Collins and although he could in no way be considered violent, enough was enough. He moved quickly forward before Raheem and his friends could do anything, grabbed the driver by the scruff of the neck and shouted: 'Get your hands on that damn wheel!' From that point on, there was silence. Nothing was said about the incident and the whole team arrived safely.

The match was one with an unexpected result. Not for Tony and Alan but for the Shah and other Persepolis fans who had pre-empted the result by laying on a massive after-game banquet to celebrate the expected victory over Bristol City. The tactic of the match was simple; 'Let the ball do the work' and it was successful, bringing with it a 1–0 defeat for the Iranians. Needless to say, the after match banquet was cancelled.

~~~~

Tony had now become established in the world of football as the 'master spy', and full feature articles focusing on his work were being written by those close to the game, such as Simon Faber. In a full page spread in the *Football Weekly News* entitled 'Bristol's Long Distance Man'. He confirmed Collins arrival at Ashton Gate in 1967 when he first joined Alan Dicks, and their need to build a new team. The youngsters who were to become stars at Bristol such as Gerry Gow, Tom Ritchie, John Galley and Dickie Rooks were all bought cheaply with good spotting skills from Collins and necessarily canny negotiating skills from Dicks. The partnership worked well in this process and although Tony may have had some desire to have a club of his own, he stated he would not leave Bristol until things were right!

Tony's first time at Bristol as Assistant Manager did actually begin in 1967 and lasted until June 1972, the start of the 72/73 season by which time Bristol had been dragged out of the depths of double figures in the Second Division at number 19, to enter the new season at number 8 and finish at a respectable number 4. Effort was being applied on all sides and the teamwork between Alan Dicks and Tony Collins was beginning to show results. The fortunate capture of tough Glaswegian Gerry Gow, spotted by Collins in 1969, was a typical example of how well the two straight talking men worked together and these are Tony's own words describing attempts to sign him.

'*I'll never forget the night Alan Dicks and myself tried to sign Gerry Gow, the bustling, aggressive midfield player for Bristol City. I thought it would cost us our lives. Gerry's father, Jim, was a docker in Scotland; rough and ready, strong as a lion, with three days stubble on his face. You didn't mess with that kind of bloke, but he seemed to take a shine to us for some reason.*

We had first seen Gow playing in a Youth Cup final and what a player he looked. His tackling was tremendous and he looked as though he wasn't afraid of anyone or anything. I made a remark to Alan when a guy standing in front of us turned round and said "You can forget him, he's tied up ... you won't get him." So I replied "I suggest you mind your own business ... I'm having a private conversation." The guy didn't know whether to say more or just leave. The warning bells rang loudly and both Alan and myself knew there and then we would have to act fast to have any chance of signing him.

We saw Gerry's dad afterwards and he told us to go and discuss the situation with him. That seemed alright but what we weren't expecting was all the family's relations to be there, about nine I think, or so it seemed at the time.

We had arranged to meet in this Glasgow pub and pubs tend to be tough places in Glasgow. This one was no exception! Alan Dicks and I walked in to find sawdust on the floor and some darting, suspicious eyes giving us the old one-two up and down as we set foot inside the place. I'm not saying it wasn't friendly – it was just that the icy stares threatened your feet with frostbite.

Dicks and I walked into this place dressed to the nines. As soon as we entered, everyone stopped talking and turned to look. Dicks shot an expression of panic in my direction and said: "Hey, they think we are the police!"

"In that case," I replied, "buy them all a bloody drink, quick!"

That changed everything. The place lit up and we had our chat. We got our man, too. Gerry Gow proved a great signing for the club.'

However, things in the boardroom were a little less calm and the battle, as always, was over money. Two directors had resigned over the issue, despite the average age of the side being lowered by some 10 years, and a profit of over £35,000 having been made on the transfer of players. By Second Division standards, Tony and Alan were working with very little money and Tony commented at the time:

'The most they ever paid is £35,000 for Bobby Kellard. To my way of looking at it, if Bristol City are to get into the First Division, their thinking will have to change substantially!'

But what about the ones that got away? Were there any real: 'I wish I hadn't done that!' moments? Well, in the process of looking at literally hundreds of players every year, there are bound to be some regrets and perhaps one of the biggest was missing out on signing Kevin Keegan for Bristol City in 1971. The situation is described here in Tony's own words.

'I'll never forget the night I first saw Kevin Keegan play football. Boundary Park at Oldham was not the plushest of grounds in the Football League, nor the warmest, but by the end of 90 minutes seeing this slip of a lad named Keegan, who no-one had ever heard of, I felt as warm as if I'd supped half a dozen brandies.

Keegan was playing for Fourth Division side Scunthorpe against Oldham; an anonymous player in an anonymous match. But when that final whistle blew, I knew I'd seen a great player in the making. I didn't care that no-one shared my optimism that night, or so I thought. I wasn't worried that this Keegan wasn't already at one of the big clubs in the North such as Liverpool, Manchester United or City. That didn't matter. It was quite usual to find some pretty good players hanging around the lower leagues in those days. The big clubs had so much competition for places in their junior ranks that lots of big name future stars slipped through the net. That was the fun and excitement of my job. I walked out of Boundary Park that night in search of a telephone box. I called up Alan Dicks and said "I've just seen a brilliant kid; what do you think? He looks a real gem!" Alan and I were looking for five or six players at the time because City were bottom of the Second Division when we went there. We still only had £25,000 to spend to find them but it was possible to find players at 'sensible' prices in those days. Alan was enthusiastic on the phone and said: "Look, get back here and we'll have a chat about him in the morning.

The next day, I gave Dicks my report. "This Keegan is a sharp, brave little lad. He gets up in the air ever so well for his size and he's as brave as a lion!" So we rang up Scunthorpe and I spoke to my old mate Ron Ashman, whom I'd played alongside at Norwich years earlier. He gave us the low down. "This lad's got it alright," confirmed Ashman. "£25,000 and he's yours, and it will be money well spent!" I came off the phone and told Dicks. His reaction surprised me.

"Let's go and buy him, now!" he said.

My reply will haunt me for the rest of my life. "No, I've only seen him once. Let's wait and have another look when he plays next." We did respect Ron Ashman but didn't want to take anyone's word on buying a player and besides, we needed so many payers at that time.

Dicks said: "Well, alright, but let's have a good look when he plays next and if he makes out, we'll buy him there and then." I felt that was fair enough. So we arranged a few days later to go and watch Keegan on the Saturday and conclude a deal that night, if he measured up to expectations. I rang Ron Ashman to tell him we were coming up.

"You needn't waste your time, Liverpool came in early this morning for him and they've agreed £25,000. He's going to Anfield," was the reply.

Every time I saw Keegan after that I wondered what could have been. We were seemingly first in; we had the opportunity. But then that's the game. Some you win and some you lose and others … you fall flat on your face!'

So the victors of the day were Chief Scout Geoff Twentyman and

Liverpool manager Bill Shankley. The figure for the 20 year old Kevin Keegan was stated at the time to be £35,000 rather than £25,000 as recalled by Tony, but actual amounts paid against those published in the press were often exaggerated for public consumption in the hope of raising a higher price when selling a player on.

By the summer of that year, 1972, things were happening at Leeds United, a successful First Division team sitting at number two in the League, a nudge behind Derby County who were winners of the FA Cup and managed by the 'marmite' … love him or hate him … figure of Brian Clough. The manager of Leeds was someone whose statue stands proudly outside the Elland Road ground of the club to this day and his name was Don Revie. He had been in charge for 11 years and his team would be voted as one of the greatest football teams of all time. Clough did not think so and he voiced his often uncalled for opinion at every opportunity in newspaper columns and television interviews.

Against a background of regular boardroom upsets at Bristol, Tony became a wanted man; wanted by Don Revie as part of his amazing backroom squad, researching and spotting players and feeding information to the manager. Leeds United had not risen from near bankruptcy in the early 60s to the dizzying heights of number 2 in the First Division by operating a pitch philosophy of 'brute force and ignorance'. Contrary to popular belief and derogatory statements made by Clough, Don Revie was a thinker, a tactician and he held a long standing admiration for Tony Collins and his attitude to the game. He did not condone brutality on the pitch but he did support determination to chase the ball, at whatever cost, and win the game. His feeling was that if that was not the all consuming objective, then there was no point in being on the pitch. For all that Clough had to say, fate would very shortly knock on his door when he would be given the opportunity to go to Leeds United and put whatever he felt was wrong there … right.

So, the call finally came for a move from Bristol. Collins commented that he was leaving what he regarded as a good club for a great club. Local newspapers quoted him as saying that although he felt he had lived with a noose around his neck at City for some years, they were in fact wonderful years and he was grateful for them.

Was Alan Dicks sad to see him go? Perhaps he was, but he had his own battles to fight and the plan he and Tony had constructed was nearly unstoppable in the carefully constructed squad the assistant manager was leaving behind. They both knew that City was heading for the First Division, as long as they could complete the transfer programme they had both decided upon without interference from the board. To cast this management policy in stone, when Collins left Bristol City, the board of directors issued a statement that the club would not sell maturing players such as Tainton and Merrick. A final quote from Tony Collins as reported by Graham Russell, probably on behalf of the *Bristol Post*, was:

> *'City will have the chance in the next few years of growing towards a First Division side. But it can't be done on coppers'*

CHAPTER NINE

Mixing with the Big Boys ...

They say that all good things must come to an end, but for Tony, an exciting new set of 'good things' were about to arrive on the horizon when he finally received the call from Don Revie. The headlines by sports columnist Herbert Gillam in the *Leeds Observer*, were straightforward and to the point.

'Collins Quits City. Revie makes him Leeds' Chief Scout'

Tony simply confirmed the situation by stating that as Leeds were one of the best clubs in the world, he could not refuse. In relation to Bristol City, he said:

'Alan Dicks had a lot of faith in me, letting me work from my home in Rochdale. I think Bristol City's prospects are very bright. We have had a lot of battles to fight at Ashton Gate in the four and a half years I have been there and we have just been rewarded with a very good season'

He also made a point about finishing 8th in the league at the end of the previous season and the transfer of Chris Garland to Chelsea had topped up the City coffers by £100,000. Although he still had a year to run on his existing contract with Bristol, the board agreed to let him go to Leeds without compensation indicating the level of regard with which both the management and board at Ashton Gate held their assistant manager.

It was a big move for Tony, who up until that particular time still maintained ambitions to manage his own club. Now it was his reputation as a man of strategy and a finely tuned eye for a young player with potential that had propelled him on to the sports pages of the National Press. His name and picture appeared in print everywhere and many considered that the 'secret was now out'. Leeds not only needed to stay in the top three of the First Division, they also needed to play well and bring home some silver from Europe. So how were they going to do it? An article heading from a Leeds United, November 1974 Match Day programme may provide a clue. It describes the Leeds backroom staff and how thorough they were, even quoting an example of knowing how many lumps of sugar a player might take in his tea. It confirmed that Leeds had spent over 14 years building up information files on players and this ongoing detailed history had now become a valuable commodity.

However, although Leeds United may have captured all the secrets on British players, what did they have on European and International players?

'And when the time comes for United to check up on European opponents, United pull out their special file. Over the years, Maurice Lindley, Chief Coach Sid Owen and latterly Tony Collins have visited practically every country in Europe on spying missions. They return armed with a mass of information on United's opponents which is channelled into pre-match planning.'

As Chief Scout, Tony had a network of other trusted scouts working on his behalf all over the country. Therefore his role became more specific in researching Leeds United's forthcoming games in Europe from the state of the teams they were playing, the performance of individual players, the condition of the ground they would be playing on along with suitable Hotels and transport availability. In an interesting and revealing club magazine article a trip made by Collins to Hungary ahead of a Leeds fixture with Ujpest Dozsa was highlighted. It confirmed how valuable such a report was to the club as the two teams prepared to meet one another in European action and that this grey file was now locked securely away in one of the famous Elland Road filing cabinets. Tony recalls the trip to Hungary in notes he made on January 27th, 1977 and these are his own words:

'Spying for Europe is so different from England; the currency and language problems, different ways of running the game of football and no knowledge of opponents etc. In England, we will have seen opposing players and teams so often that even seeing them on a bad day without any real patterns emerging, we can put together a reasonably accurate report, and there is always the possibility at the time of being able to see them again before we meet them. In Europe, we have got to be right first time, especially when you take into consideration the money being spent on a trip and the prize that could be at stake.

One of my most absorbing trips was to Hungary for Leeds United to report on our second round opponents in the European Cup, Ujpest Dozsa. Generally we used to send two representatives because of the complications that can arise in a foreign country. However, we were so busy at the time, I had to go to Hungary alone and carry out three peoples job; my own, the Club Secretary and the Public Relations Officer. My day started by catching the early train from Manchester to Euston where I met Tom Saunders, the Liverpool scout. Liverpool were playing Ferencvarosi Torna, who were the opponents of Ujpest Dozsa. We then made our way to London's Heathrow airport to catch the midday flight to Budapest. We arrived at around 2.30 pm and Tom and I were met by our interpreters. Then we split up, arranging to meet again at the match. My interpreter's name was Stephen Mittler and travelling from the airport I asked to see a nice big hotel in the centre of the city so I could time the run from the airport to the hotel.

After a quick view of the hotel and being quite satisfied, I arranged to book rooms for the Directors and members of the Press. Then I asked Stephen to find a nice quiet hotel about a half hour run from our venue, the Nep Stadium. We soon arrived at the Hotel Europa and I walked around the area to try and find a small flat piece of ground nearby where we could have a short workout. Back at the hotel I ordered a room at the back of the property to test for noise and viewed a private dining or meeting room we could use for a team talk. We had just enough time for a sandwich before we had to go to the stadium as two matches were being played that evening. The first was Vasas versus Honved and then half an hour after the finish the two top Hungarian teams would meet.

I timed the run from the hotel to the stadium because we did not want to arrive too early on match day. I had to keep going on at my interpreter to get me a team listing as they did not print programmes. I managed to get hold of this vital document after a few worries and 20 minutes before kick-off. I did my report, attended a short press conference after the game and timed the run back to the hotel again. At the hotel, I tried out the steaks to make sure the food was acceptable and arranged to meet Stephen again at 7.00 am the following morning. The interpreter arrived on time and I asked him to tell the hotel management that if the band that was playing, keeping me awake until 3.00 am played that loud and that late again, then Leeds United would have to find another place to stay. I was given assurances that there would be no band when we came over for the match, so we went straight over to the Ujpest Dozsa offices in the city.

There, I had to discuss ticket allocations for Directors, players and staff and the normal exchange of presents and pennants along with the number of people coming, details of occupations and full names etc so that visas could be arranged. I asked them to call us with prices of hotel rooms etc and who would be paying for what when we came to Budapest and vice-versa when they came to Leeds. I also needed to advise them of the number of fans expected to attend from Leeds and make arrangements on my return with the British Post Office to provide enough outgoing lines for the Hungarian officials. There was work to do in collecting players pictures so that we could put together special programmes for the events from which I am told we could often make up to £90,000 from European Cup matches. I would also make arrangements to have a large pack of player pictures printed in a few suitable languages for the Ujpest Dozsa club.

All the information I required would also have to be provided to them for their visit to Leeds and I arranged for a meeting with an interpreter and club officials to discuss any queries arising from the day's talks. We agreed they would come over to England to see us play against Wolves and what we could hopefully help them with during that visit.

I had one hour to spare before catching the plane home and when I arrived, everyone asked "Did you have a good time?"

So, this kind of preparation for a football match was a step-up from the kind of lengths that many other clubs would go to in their attempts to grab hold of some trophies in Europe. In today's International game, this kind of research and attention to commercial detail is commonplace, but then, it was quite experimental, and financially relatively costly. Tony considered his days with Leeds United were in themselves exciting in his role as chief scout, although the work pressure was continuous and working days often very long. Don however always showed his appreciation for any specific work done and all positive results obtained and to a man everyone at Leeds United during Revie's reign looked forward to going to work.

Whilst at Leeds it's true to say that Tony maintained a good relationship with all the players, whose lounge was coincidentally just opposite Tony and Maurice Lindley's office. As a result, contact was close and regular and it was good that playing and non-playing staff had the opportunity to mix and get to know one another well.

One day Don Revie asked Tony if he would mind running Billy Bremner down to the FA Headquarters at Lancaster Gate for a disciplinary hearing. It concerned the number of bookings by a referee within a certain time frame. In the particular incident under investigation a match was in progress between Leeds United and Queens Park Rangers (QPR). The ball went out of play last touched by a QPR player and therefore should have been a Leeds throw-in. So in anticipation of the throw-in the Leeds players all moved forward and up the field of play to set up an attack. Suddenly, a QPR player picked up the ball and threw it to his players leaving Leeds out of place and exposed with the QPR forwards left unmarked. Obviously, the Leeds players were left feeling very hard done by. They surrounded the referee and linesman to complain and in the ensuing confusion, Billy Bremner was booked. Was it fair that only one man was booked out of the gaggle of players surrounding the officials ... and was it fair that this person was singled out to be Bremner ... that was the question? By booking Bremner it meant he had now accumulated too many bookings and would have to explain himself before an FA disciplinary board. The result could have been a three match suspension and he would therefore miss the last crucial games of the season. Don told Tony he said he wouldn't really have to say anything because as far as Don was concerned; 'We've got no chance!'

When Tony and Billy arrived at Lancaster Gate all the press were there and as the smiling pair were walking in, a passing taxi driver wound down his window and shouted 'Good luck Billy – hope you get off!'

In the days before mobile phones, unless a telephone happened to be nearby, then receiving urgent messages was often quite difficult. However, the press of the day had their own communications source and one of them told Tony that Don Revie wanted him to ring. He found a phone and spoke to Don who asked if Tony could defend Billy. Tony states that he didn't even know the detail of the charge surrounding the event but agreed to do what he could and was left reading the case notes as he was about to enter the building. When he arrived with Bremner in the hearing room Tony noticed the disciplinary board was made up of quite a few club directors that he knew well. The time came when Billy and Tony, as his representative, were asked if they would like to defend the charge, so Tony quickly stood up and told the board that they hadn't come to have a go at the referee and linesman, because the whole affair was simply a case of mistaken identity. Billy was definitely not the person who should have been booked. The board whispered amongst themselves for a couple of minutes and finally announced with some sense of relief that the charge had been dropped.

So when they came out of Lancaster Gate the 'press boys' wanted to know the verdict and what had been said. Tony pushed his way through with Billy close by his side providing a brush-off comment to the hacks; 'We can't stop ... we've got to get back!' When free of the clamouring reporters, they rang Don Revie and told him what had happened. Surprisingly, he just offered a one word reply delivered with little enthusiasm. Tony thought it a little strange and didn't wish to extend the conversation over the phone. However, when they got back Don was absolutely ecstatic; he couldn't believe it. Leeds were vying for the championship that year with only three games left and if Billy had received a likely three match ban, then this could have been catastrophic for Leeds chances. Billy Bremner was so impressed with Tony's performance at the hearing he seriously asked Tony if he would become his agent.

~~~~

The off-field operations could well be compared to a series of spying missions where everything was top secret and kept solely within the club. Everyone wanted to know what Leeds were doing and if even the smallest hint of 'who and where' leaked to the press, then player prices could become inflated due to the speculation.

In a Soccer Special article by Alan Thompson in the *Daily Express* newspaper of Friday March 31st, 1975, the headline was:

Master Spies! – *'Leeds launch campaign to conquer Europe'*

This article looked in depth at the activities of Tony Collins, Chief Scout, Maurice Lindley, Assistant Manager and Syd Owen, Chief Coach, now known as the 'backroom boys' at Leeds United. After some success in Belgium against Anderlecht in the march toward lifting the European Cup with the revealing sub-headline confirming 'The path Leeds United tread in Europe – and the men who aim to make it a little smoother ...'

The journalist sang the praises of Leeds with a record in Europe of 41 games, 17 wins, 15 draws and 9 losses. He put such success down to pre-match planning and the activities of Collins and the other members of the front line team. When interviewed in an article titled 'Soccer Chat' by Don Evans, Don Revie was said to have made the following comment.

> Don disclaims much of the credit. *'You must have a bit of luck riding with you and great credit goes to Maurice Lindley, Tony Collins and the scouting system.'*

At that time, Revie had the United first team squad insured for a nearly unheard of amount of £2.5 million, probably equivalent to around £45 million at today's values (2015). The major purchases had been Allan Clarke, Mick Jones and Trevor Cherry. Interestingly, what were referred to as the nursery side put together by Collins and Lindley include some names that were destined to become famous both in the UK and Europe such as David Harvey, Billy Bremner, Norman Hunter, Paul Madeley, Frankie Gray, Terry Yorath and Peter Lorimer.

Leeds United, the way it was managed and its enviable record of successes, meant that manager Don Revie, who had been shepherding the team since 1961, was being mooted as the next England team manager and following the 1973–74 season, he left to take up the position vacated by Alf Ramsey in July 1974. Everyone was looking for a repeat performance as provided in the 1966 World Cup event, but in 1974, England had failed to qualify and so a sensible Ramsey agreed to bow out quietly.

The kind of football Leeds United played did not go down well with many of the more conservative English clubs; in fact they were hated by most. They played a fast paced game described as 'suffocating' their opponents and 'overwhelming' other players who tried to pass around them. If a side they were playing kicked the players more than the ball, then you could be sure that Leeds would kick back. It was said that they harassed officials and physically attacked opponents on the field. However, the kind of night many Leeds fans remember is when they were truly on top of their game beating Southampton 7-0 and keeping the ball for 39 consecutive passes.

This match was one of the rare occasions when the new football dedicated programme 'Match of the Day' had its cameras on hand to record the extraordinary outcome and thanks to modern media availability the amazing moves made by Leeds United can still be seen on YouTube to the shouts by Leeds fans of 'Ole, Ole' as their players simply ran rings around the opposition. 'It's almost cruel' were the words used by commentator Barry Davies, confirming that Leeds were putting on a 'brilliant show' with the opposing team apparently not really on the park.

Lorimer noted that it was a period when Leeds United were 'slamming' most teams and Don Revie, who was in fact a disciplinarian, had total belief in the team and allowed the players to go out onto the park and 'do their own thing!' The Southampton match would become folklore with rumours that after the 7th goal, Revie asked the lads to try and not score any more. With Johnny Giles and Billy Bremner in midfield, Eddie Gray in top form and Allan 'Sniffer' Clarke up front ready to 'knock 'em in', then such a goal scoring machine, on that particular day would be difficult to stop.

The reputation of tough unforgiving play did unfortunately spread at times to the terraces at Leeds Games with some sections of supporters often being as feared as much off the pitch as some would say the team was on it. George Best was said to have claimed the only games he needed to wear shin-pads was when facing Leeds United and this was not an uncommon muttering amongst many of the First Division sides.

~~~~

So as Revie left in 1974 to take over the England team, the new manager walking through the door at Elland Road finally turned out to be Brian Clough. When Revie made the decision to leave United the directors were perhaps caught napping and Manny Cussins, the chairman made his first approach to Jock Stein who was in charge of Celtic at the time. He turned the job down and it is understood he pointed Cussins in the direction of a young and talented manager, Ian St John, who was quite happily settled at Scottish club Motherwell. A meeting at Scotch Corner on the A1 appeared to go well although Clough was still a last place candidate, and one the chairman wished to speak with. What really happened between Cussins and Clough will remain a mystery but when all the cards were dealt, it was Clough who came up with a winning hand. Was Clough an expected replacement for Revie? No! Was he a welcome replacement to Revie by the staff and players at Leeds? No!

No one on the staff and especially those in the 'backroom' thought he would last long but only 44 days was something of a record in English football. The mystery remains as to why he took the job in the first place especially as he and his assistant Peter Taylor had a job offer at Brighton & Hove Albion, according to the film of the event titled 'The Damned United'. However, the mistake he made in this particular move was probably not to have the calming influence of Peter Taylor with him in the dressing room, as Clough was a vehement critic of Leeds United, the way they played football and the man who was still known there as the 'boss'!

He hated Revie and all he stood for and made no bones about it. It was an obviously unsettling time for the team and the staff at Elland Road. To Clough, the club considered themselves to be 'Revie's club' and he was the last man anyone there wanted to have contact with and so someone with a more settling influence was chosen to replace him. It is estimated the pay-off to Clough was just short of six figures and he seemingly boasted about the fact to journalists who met with him on the day of his sacking. He was to say later the sum he received at that time set him up for life financially ... and it probably did. More about the controversial 'Cloughie' later!

Jimmy Armfield took over the reins in October, 1974 and would stay in charge until the end of the 1977–78 season. Under his careful eye, Leeds would not perform spectacularly but they would remain in the top ten of the Football League; reach the European Cup Final in 1975 where they lost to Bayern Munich 2-0, play in the FA Cup semi-finals and the League Cup semi-finals. Armfield remembers in a Yorkshire Post article in March 2008 that he had a 'soft spot' for Leeds as a club and he also liked the city. He noted that the people there were 'very good to me' and generally, in his time at Elland Road, he thought he had done well.

With Armfield in charge, the regular spies were hard at work. In the race to get the upper hand in the European Cup he said that Barcelona had already been watched and that Maurice, Syd and Tony would be clocking up a lot of miles and flying hours in the following weeks.

In a European Cup Special by Alan Thompson of the *Daily Express*, the fierce, physical battle between Leeds and Barcelona was described in detail. There was also a joint article titled 'Spies bring good cheer' with a photo beneath showing Tony Collins, *Daily Express* reporter Derek Potter and Leeds United Assistant Manager, Maurice Lindley. All of them had been absent at the Leeds-Barcelona confrontation where Joe Jordan walked off the field in a shirt covered with blood. They had in fact been at the Bayern Munich match to witness the beating of St. Etienne 2-0 giving them enough confidence to announce ...

'Leeds United can follow Manchester United and win the European Cup in Paris on May 28th. The way for a British victory is wide open'

Judging by the way the team not only survived, but won convincingly against Barcelona with only ten men, the pundits and spies could well be proven right. And who was there to savour the victory? It could only have been one man; Don Revie, England manager who was the last man to leave the directors box with his arms around the club chairman Manny Cussins. However, the game of football that was to follow that victorious evening left little room for celebration by anyone on any team ... and here is how the game went from Tony's point of view.

The European Cup Final that took place in Paris on May 28th, 1975 would go down as one the greatest injustices in the history of professional football. Leeds United were scheduled to play Bayern Munich. The referee was a Frenchman named Michel Kitabdjian and before the game was over, he would have a lot to answer for. Some great names were on the pitch such as Franz Beckenbauer, Franz Roth and Gerd Muller for Munich and Peter Lorimer, Billy Bremner, Johnny Giles and Alan Clarke for Leeds. In the first half, two legitimate penalty appeals were rejected by the referee despite a blatant foul on Clarke by Beckenbauer. In the second half a well placed volley by Lorimer was all for nothing as the referee declared an off-side offence on Bremner. Initially, Kitabdjian awarded a goal and then rescinded it.

The final result was a 2–0 win for Munich with all hell breaking loose at the Leeds end of the ground. Anger also spilled over onto the streets of Paris with some Leeds fans looking to find an outlet for their frustrations. The team were left physically and emotionally decimated with no Don Revie to pull them round again. Was this dreadful defeat possibly the start of the real rot at Elland Road? More in a moment, but obviously there were some critics that thought it could be and despite accusations of match fixing by Kitabdjian the result stood and Leeds United had to settle for second place in Europe that year. Tony made his opinions known within football, that a referee taking charge of his last ever professional game at such an important tie should never be offered the job. The reasoning was simple. Such a situation would leave an official possibly open to bribery if they had nothing to lose with a career that would end with the final whistle anyway!

~~~~

Tony Collins and Don Revie had a close relationship and one that had grown over the years to become even closer during Tony's time at Leeds United. Before leaving the club, Revie wrote some personal letters to Tony and the following one is dated May 13th, 1974.

Dear Tony,

Just a short note to say a very sincere "thank you" for all the hard work you have put in throughout the season on behalf of our club.

Without your help and assistance we would not be able to run our club so competently, and I would like to assure you that your efforts are greatly appreciated.

Best wishes and thank you again.

Yours sincerely

A further one, noting his departure from Leeds was dated July 16th, 1974.

Dear Tony,

First of all let me say how sorry and sad I am to be leaving this Club, and particularly you, Tony, and the rest of the staff.

My taking the England job possibly reflects great credit on you and the rest of the staff for the way you have dedicated yourselves and worked for me.

Without you we could not have achieved what we did in the past.

I will miss you very much, and if ever I can help you in any way you know you only have to pick up the phone or drop me a line.

Thank you again for all the hard work and dedication you put in, and I am sure you will give the next manager exactly the same co-operation.

Yours very sincerely,'

However, the association of these two men at 'the top of their game' was not to end there. With permission from the Leeds board, Tony Collins became the Master Spy for the England team as well as Leeds United. The unsettling episode of Brian Clough's appearance at Elland Road had made many nervous and therefore no objection was raised to Tony doing work for Don Revie on a personal basis. He writes another letter to Tony on November 19th of the same year.

Dear Tony,

Thank you for the wonderful breakdown of the England performance against Czechoslovakia. I will be sending your expenses off in the next 10 days.

Give our love to Edith – hope things go well for the old Club.

Yours sincerely.

Signed: Don Revie.

England Team Manager'

During the period of Jimmy Armfield's tenure as manager, the biggest match of everyone's life simply had to be the European Cup final. Leeds should have won it of course, and they clearly could have won it, but fate and a referee with a possible eye problem steered the silverware in the direction of Bayern Munich. The headline in the *Weekly News* of June 7th, 1975 by an unidentified reporter was:

'The Cup that got away'... and Joe Jordan, in a newspaper column where he attempted to explain the reason for their defeat, stated *'I Hold My Hands Up To You, Franz Beckenbauer'*. He also could not fathom how Leeds United could lose a match they 'bossed for 75 minutes!' On the same page, it was noted that the search for new players had begun in earnest.

'If there are any more about like McQueen ...?' and it was Tony Collins who was being asked the question.

'Chief scout Tony Collins is the man saddled with the job of underwriting the future of Leeds United. The Elland Road club have no prototype in mind when they chase young talent, but if there are any kids around like centre-half Gordon McQueen they will get the Collins recommendation'

Tony knew the fight was on stating that *'ability is a must of course, but I would put character as another priority'*. He also knew what the devastating result against Bayern meant when he said:

'Leeds are always chasing success. This means there can be some fierce disappointments like the European Cup final. That is where character to bounce back is essential and Gordon has that'

However, the disappointment at such a failure seemed to have an effect on the team who would never again dominate the game of English Football as they had done in the Revie era. In Tony's eyes, perhaps the buzz had gone, something was missing and although he had a good relationship with Jimmy Armfield, he knew it was time to move on.

Two other 'backroom boys' at Elland Road had already moved on. They were chief coach Syd Owen and trainer Les Cocker. There had been rumours for some time that people would have to go and although Tony Collins had 18 months of his contract still to run, he knew the writing was firmly on the wall. He commented at the time:

'When Syd left it was made clear that the board no longer believed in staff contracts. Syd helped build the club into the power it is today. If they can let a fellow like that go after 15 years because of a contract what chance, I thought, would I as a relative new boy of the backroom staff have?'

He added:

'I have my wife and family to think about, so I had no alternative but to look to the future!'

The future, of course, turned out to be a short step back into the past when he signed a contract as Assistant Manager to Alan Dicks once again at Second Division Bristol City in the December of 1975. The job consisted of a very suitable salary of £5,000 and three year tenure with some substantial bonuses if the club returned to the First Division once more. Best of all, Tony was back amongst friends and it was seen as a measure of respect that he had been able to take up a place at Ashton Gate again and the club were definitely getting geared up for a promotion challenge.

At Leeds, Jimmy Armfield stated publicly that he was sorry to see him go. There were rumours of course that the replacement of Syd Owen with former Arsenal Chief Coach, Don Howe had proved a bad match with Collins, and this new addition to the coaching staff at Elland Road had pushed Tony into the move to Bristol. However, both Armfield and Collins deny any bad blood between them with Armfield stating:

'The club would have been prepared to discuss terms with Tony when his contract was due to run out in 18 months' ... but the decision had been made ... and so the matter was laid to rest.

So, Bristol City were now going places with the effective team of Dicks and Collins firmly back in place. The 1974-75 season had seen the club sit comfortably at number 5 in the Second Division and both the manager and assistant manager knew they had the team to take them to the top. Don Revie, however, still needed Tony to scout and report and a suitable sabbatical arrangement was made with the England manager and Dicks to let Tony loose on Europe when required. In a 1976 article from an unidentified newspaper of the day by a similarly unidentified reporter, this commentator noted the following:

Rome Date For Ex-Manager — *' Collins, the former Rochdale manager, will be in the official England party for next Wednesday's World Cup qualifying match against Italy in Rome.'*

The report confirmed that Tony had been invited by Don Revie, the England manager to join the team in Rome. It noted that this could be regarded in some way as a thank you from Don for Tony's watching and reporting on International matches between Finland-Sweden and Italy-Romania. He was asked by the reporter to give forth on a possible final result of the match but a sensible Tony Collins simply stated that the match would be hard and the Italians are supremely skilful players.

With a concentrated effort required at Bristol City and certain responsibilities with the England team, Tony Collins was destined to be a very busy man for the following twelve months! There was always the call from the England manager to be listened to of course and on March 5th, 1976 Don Revie wrote:

'Dear Tony,

The matches I would like you to cover for me are as follows:-

Wednesday, 19th May, Finland v Switzerland at KUPIO 6.30 pm K.O.

Tuesday, 1st June, Finland v Sweden at HELSINKI 7.00 pm K.O.

I would also possibly like you to watch Italy v Romania in Italy, Tony, but I don't have details of this match yet, apart from the date which is 5th June. I will arrange for Tomas Cook's in London to send you plane tickets and flight times for the games in Finland.

Cars will be laid on to take you from the airport to the stadiums and I will also arrange for you to receive £..... worth of traveller's cheques for each game. I will book you into the hotel we will be using and perhaps you could check up on the facilities available, training grounds, etc.

I do appreciate you doing this for me, Tony, very much indeed, as it is so vital that we get a good result on the 13th June, which will get us away to a good start.'

Not knowing what lay round the corner, there were many things going on at Bristol that could be considered distractions. However, Tony Collins knew that the search for new, young players with potential would be critical for Bristol to climb up the division and with boardroom disruptions continuing and finances stretched due to high legal costs, both he and Alan Dicks were rightly concerned.

CHAPTER TEN

When in Doubt ... Move On!

Alan Dicks knew well that the work both he and Tony had put in during their previous partnership together at Bristol should be about to pay off ... big time! Keeping the atmosphere calm within the club was now the key to success in maintaining a tangible excitement in the air, with attendances up for every game at Ashton Gate. The team, captained by Geoff Merrick were gradually climbing up the league ladder. Some likened Merrick to Bobby Moore in terms of talent, style and the ability to lead from the front. He had been spotted by Dicks and Collins as a young 18 year old England boy's player and captain of the Bristol boy's team. From the time, some several years earlier, that Dicks and Collins had begun their long term plan to put together a young, tactical side unsullied by too much time with the bruisers of the sport, things had started to happen at Ashton Gate, and now was payback time. Of course, much was still reliant upon a receptive and supportive boardroom to finance the team and the facilities at Ashton Gate. Unfortunately, the board of Bristol City F.C. were still more concerned with politics and in-fighting than getting 'with the plan' ... and although the unsettling aggravation did sometimes filter its way down to the operational staff, Alan and Tony did their best to ensure it didn't get as far as the dressing room.

The near quarter of a million pound stand that previous chairman Harry Dolman had built turned into a financial millstone firmly fixed round the club's neck. Robert Hobbs the chairman of the time made attempts to pour oil on troubled waters, and to keep the banks at bay he needed high numbers through the turnstiles with large amounts of cash ringing in the tills.

Tony was still very much involved with the England team of course and suitable leave arrangements had been made with Bristol to give Don Revie the freedom to make use of his services.

Fortune was now smiling on Dicks, witnessing some excellent match results with Tom Ritchie up at the front joined by Paul Cheesley. These two would become a great partnership and by the end of October 1975, City would be leading the Second Division and looking promotion firmly in the face. By the spring of the following year, home gates of 22,000 and 23,000 were being seen regularly and local businesses were also seeing the effect. Everyone seemed to be walking round with a smile on their face in Bristol and when promotion came at the end of the season, the team and the fans knew it had all been worth it. With seemingly stable finances, good gates and a feeling of well being about the place, Ashton Gate was to witness its first games as a top flight football club for some 65 years. But dark clouds lay just over the horizon in an unnecessarily expensive boardroom upheaval in 1977 where Hobbs was to be removed as chairman and a protracted, drawn out litigation would see the lawyers richer and the club much poorer because of it.

There was also the Duncan McKenzie situation for Tony Collins to deal with; a sort of 'harp back' to the whirlwind devastation caused by the Clough visitation at Leeds United. In the *News of the World* sports pages of September 12th, 1976 nestled an entry titled "Duncan McKenzie's own story", there was a claim concerning Tony's involvement in some sort of meeting with McKenzie and two other players brought to Leeds from Derby by Clough in his short tenure as manager. There were some claims that discrimination against the ex-Derby players was afoot. Tony quickly stamped on the situation by writing to the *News of the World* Sports Editor on September 20th, threatening legal action and demanding a withdrawal. The newspaper's legal department chewed the matter over for a month and on October 20th, sent a reply confirming a suitable retraction and an offer to pay Tony's legal costs in the matter.

However, for Tony Collins, with the short McKenzie confrontation now behind him, he knew there was work to do with his first division side. 1977 would be a memorable year for many reasons; the first year in the First Division, the fierce boardroom battle at Ashton Gate and a testimonial match for the Assistant Manager. It was quite unusual to provide what was in fact an honour to non-playing management staff of a football club and was much appreciated by the man it was designed to impress. The game would be Bristol City against an England Eleven which Tony would choose and included some great players of the day such as Peter Shilton, Tony Currie, Paul Mariner, Stan Bowles and Trevor Francis amongst others. Attendance for the match at Ashton Gate was a respectable six and a half thousand and the result was a crowd pleasing England 6, Bristol City 4. The players all received from Tony the valued 'must have' gift of an engraved onyx cigarette lighter as unfortunately smoking was the necessary social accessory in the 1970s. The date of the testimonial was September 20th and the account presented to Tony showed the final amount raised after expenses, was £5,849.10, a substantial figure at today's values (2015). The audience for this very special game included many celebrities of the day such as Elton John, who was a well known pop star and chairman of Watford. Elton and Tony had a relationship going back some years with the common bond being simply football. For some who could not make it, like Paul Madeley who suffered a weekend injury, there were letters and telegrams of congratulations. The one from Don Revie read:

'Best wishes for tonight Tony. Hope all goes well and no one deserves it more'

Headlines on page 15 of the *Evening Post* dated Wednesday September 21st, 1977 as reported by Peter Godsiff stated: *"Ashton game 'useful' for Greenwood"* confirming that the England manager Ron Greenwood turned up for the testimonial match and ended up taking charge of the team. He described the match as being, '... a breathtaking exhibition of ball skills and individual artistry from some of the top players in the land and an enjoyable, satisfying game.'

Ron later told reporters he would reject suggestions that it was in any way an artificial game because there would be less hard contact and tackling than in competitive matches. Peter Godsiff quoted Greenwood as saying:

'It wasn't pansy stuff. Some of the goals wouldn't have been stopped even if there had been 'knuckle' there. They showed people they can play'

With Clive Thomas officiating on the pitch, the match was understandably well managed. For Tony and Edith, the whole event was quite moving and a public stamp of approval from a sport ... and a business that Tony Collins, football's master spy, had devoted his life to for over 50 years.

The summer of 1977 had brought with it the inevitable chase for new players and the staving off of tempting offers for star members of the team such as Merrick, Tainton, Collier, Gow, Ritchie, Gillies and Sweeny etc. Although Dicks and Collins found themselves in the enviable position of having over 30 first squad members to pick a team from each week, memories of the Arsenal attempt to grab Ritchie and Merrick a couple of seasons previously for £250,000 were still haunting the two managers with a jittery board wanting to accept a deal and the fans saving the day by buying season tickets early to push a further £60,000 into the accounts.

With the Collins philosophy being seen to work at Bristol, and in effect being given long enough for the result to play out, both he and Dicks knew that the position they were now in was no simple event of chance. Catching young talent, buying them cheap, training them in the ways and skills of a team to work around opposition players and remain un-injured, with a big enough squad to choose from in case anyone got unlucky was the mantra … and it had worked!

Unfortunately, there were some grievous misfortunes to come with Cheesley playing in his second match of the club's first season in the First Division. He made an airborne challenge to Peter Shilton of Stoke City and landed with his knee exposed to some irreparable ligament damage and he was never to play for the Ashton Gate side again.

Bristol ended their first season in the First Division at 18th position and had managed to survive. It was a different and more relentless level of football and the young ambitious side evidently had what it took to stay there. Now a plan was required to ensure that not only would Bristol remain in the First Division, they would climb to the very top … and with what they had, including perhaps a few additions, both Alan Dicks and Tony Collins thought it was possible. However, the boardroom battles continued thereby creating an uncomfortable atmosphere throughout the club. It was one that hung relentlessly over the fortunes of Bristol City and could only be considered as disconcerting for managers and players alike. Whatever financial vacuum the finances were seen to be in, it certainly could not be put down to extravagance on the pitch. Between them, Collins and Dicks had spent only £116,000 on players to get Bristol City into the First Division ... and in 1977 that took some doing!

There were of course other honours to be chased in the form of silverware, claiming victory in the Anglo-Scottish Cup tournament during the 1977–78 season. Bristol met St. Mirren in the final (managed at the time by a young, moody Alex Ferguson) and won the trophy on an aggregate score of 3–2, played over two legs. Ferguson would become a well known but possibly controversial figure in English soccer and both he and Tony Collins would meet again under some very different circumstances.

In February 1979, James Mossop would write in the Sunday Express: *'Bristol City's "bargains" challenge the big boys'*. The article praises Alan Dicks for his work in dragging the club up through to the First Division stating that under Dicks, Bristol City had become one of the games modest success stories. He also gives credit where he feels it due, stating that behind many of the signings must lay the shrewd, talent spotting eye of Tony Collins, the assistant manager. He raised further awareness that Tony lived some 200 miles away in the heart of some of England's 'most fertile footballing country at Rochdale in Lancashire'. Shrewd is definitely the right word to describe moves instigated by Collins of goalkeeper John Shaw and midfielder Jimmy Mann from Leeds United for free. He was also instrumental in bringing in Norman Hunter for £40,000 and Terry Cooper for a measly £10,000. Mossop states that Dicks leaves Collins to roam at will. His ear stays close to the transfer market gossip and as soon as Hunter became available in the break-up of the formidable Leeds team, he was ready to pounce.

Hunter wrote a quite revealing article in the series 'Norman Hunters World' with the headline *'Manager's job not for me – but I'd like to teach kids'*. He wrote about Tony who had had an effect on him in the years they had known one another. He described him as someone who has exceptionally good knowledge of the game and can assess a player's strengths and weaknesses leaving him as one of the most respected men in professional football. Thinking back to his Leeds United days, Norman Hunter recalls the effect Tony had on the team.

> *'The value of a man like Tony is illustrated by just one deal he set up. He told the boss (Revie) that there was only one centre half in Britain with the potential to take over from Jack Charlton.'*

He then went on to relate the story about Gordon McQueen, who was at the time a raw young player with Scottish side St Mirren. On Tony's recommendation Revie paid about £35,000 for McQueen and then he was later sold on to Manchester United for almost half a million. He continued:

> *'When I was chatting to Tony recently, he told me that at one time it was easy to sign quality defenders at reasonable prices. But now they have become scarce'*

Following promotion to the First Division, Bristol City continued to make headway ending up 18th at the end of the 76-77 season, 17th a year later and 13th at the end of 1979. Boardroom tensions however, could no longer be contained within the management offices of Ashton gate and started to spill out onto the field. An account of what was going on appeared as headlines in the *Bristol Evening Post* on Wednesday 12th November, 1980 … and it did not make pretty reading as it was announced: *'Bristol City Hit By 'Who's Boss?' Row'*

The reporter was Peter Godsiff and he told it as it was. A special shareholders meeting had been called the night before, the newspaper claimed, and the description of events included 'amazing scenes' as it went on to illustrate the battle between Stephen Kew, the current chairman and Robert Hobbs, still nursing wounds from his 1977 ousting as chairman. The report stated that five directors and their legal advisers had walked out on the 200 shareholders in attendance. They in turn voted off five directors being Kew, Norman Jones, Harry Bissex, Peter West and Malcolm Fox. Those voted on were Hobbs, Leslie Kew (a distant relative of Stephen Kew), Fred Mathews, John Drinkwater and Dennis Squires. The leader of the so called 'rebel' shareholders, Lionel Amos could not become a director due to a libel action pending against the board.

As anyone could see, even from Godsiff's very short and concise recording of events, and leaving aside individual personalities, the situation at board level for Bristol City was a serious one, ending up with a Football League enquiry into the club's affairs at their own instigation and Stephen Kew back in the driving seat as chairman.

The lead up to this sorry state of affairs was the relegation of Bristol City back to the second division at the end of the 79–80 season. There was to be a natural scapegoat of course in the form of a frustrated Alan Dicks. He was called to a board meeting in September to answer for the situation. Tony met him on the stairs as he exited the meeting. The news was that he had been offered the job of General Manager – but without responsibility for the team. This offer of course was totally ridiculous and quickly rejected. Within hours he was gone and it was Tony's turn next.

He had written several pages of notes to form part of a statement to the board. He was rightly quite angry at the way Alan Dicks had been treated and eventually told them he had an offer from Leeds

United to go back as Chief Scout, but under the terms of his contract there would be an entitlement to compensation for loss of services. Kew told Tony that he felt there was a correct way of 'doing things' and therefore he would have to contact the Leeds chairman. Tony reminded Mr Kew that no compensation had been asked for by Leeds during his move back to Bristol and that under the terms of his contract, he could force Bristol to pay him five years salary – if he was pushed out. Tony's ethic however was work, not sitting out some compensation payment period so he made the offer to forego his compensation claim. However, in return if the club asked Leeds for one single penny, then he would simply stay where he was to the very end of his contract and become a club embarrassment. The board eventually backed down with two directors apologising to Tony making the excuse they originally backed the idea because of the club's finances. Tony replied sharply:

'You've no need to tell me anything about the club's finances!'

It appeared difficult to get over to the directors of the club that until they got their act together, nothing could improve on the field of play, no matter how good the individual players were. The board members had completely lost sight of the fact that football is a team game, and team spirit and co-operation is not confined to an area within some white lines on a grass field. It has to extend from the bottom to the very top and with the possibility of many costly lawsuits continuing to be fought at the highest level, then there was little hope for what had once been a simply brilliant team.

Bristol City in the Autumn of 1980 had more or less completely lost the plot. They were now relegated back to the Second Division with the new shadow board still talking about guaranteeing sums of around £100,000 to get back into the First Division again. However, a possibly more informed opinion warned that a figure of £3 million would not be enough to get them back on top ... and both Dicks and Collins had alerted the board to the forthcoming situation more than a year or so before.

From Tony's viewpoint the club had been strangled due to lack of finance for new players and the refusal of directors to put up the required guarantees. When it was confirmed in the October of 1980 that Tony was leaving Bristol, Ex-Chairman Robert Hobbs wrote him a letter dated the 28th of that month.

> *'Dear Tony,*
>
> *I read with interest your article in the Sunday People. The press stated at the commencement of the 79/80 season there would be £500,000 for Alan to spend on new players. I give you and Alan credit for not revealing the true facts. Without doubt Alan suffered through not signing new players. A fresh face is always welcomed by supporters who are very fickle.*
>
> *I wish you success in your return to Leeds and trust that one day we shall run across each other. I am too shy to say when City's decline started.*
>
> *Yours sincerely.'*

Robert Hobbs was a different animal to Stephen Kew. Hobbs came from a background of grit and dirt in the quarrying business and was not known for mincing his words. Kew came from a much different environment being an old public school type and a figure who spoke quite condescendingly to just about everyone he came in contact with. From Tony's viewpoint, the man felt himself to be slightly superior to all those around him. He liked the status of 'Chairman' and was always very hospitable to visiting directors. He also ensured that all travelling expense incurred in attending away games was covered fully by the club. He was probably one of the wealthiest directors on the Bristol City board, but was considered by Tony and Alan to be tight fisted in all his financial dealings; spending the very least on club requirements. In a newspaper article titled 'Skinflint' Tony reveals the chairman held out his hand when he left but Tony refused to shake it. He told Stephen Kew *'Your attitude has broken the link between us!'* adding *'Your tight fisted policies are the main reason why Bristol City are no longer in the First Division and will be struggling in the Second.'*

The leaving of the manager on 30th September and assistant manager on October 17th was a sad time for all concerned at Ashton Gate, with a despondent Dicks going off to rest for some time before leaving the country to manage Ethnikos Piraeus in Greece. Tony of course moved back to Leeds United with a new contract guaranteeing him £12,000 a year under the stewardship of Allan Clarke. The new manager at Bristol, Bob Houghton, wrote Tony a letter on his leaving:

' Dear Tony,

Just a short line to thank you for the assistance given to me in the short time we have worked together. I would like you to know that Roy (Roy Hodgson) and I have a very high regard for the work you have done at Bristol City and we both wish you the best of luck at Leeds. I sincerely hope we shall maintain contact in the future and shall look forward to meeting up with you again sometime during the season.

Best Wishes,

Yours sincerely'

Bob Houghton had put a brave face on a particularly precarious situation knowing he had inherited a club with little or no money, an ageing team of overpaid players and a bank manager threatening closure unless the club came up with £200,000 by the end of February

1981. He made it clear that the nonsensical situation of players on recently signed long term contracts earning near to £1,000 a week needed to end and something also needed to be done about gates that had slumped from 20,000 to often less than 8,000. However, to keep the board and the bank happy, he agreed to sell Gerry Gow to Manchester City for £275,000 – an amount that went straight to the bank. Twenty two year old mid-fielder Kevin Mabbutt was also in his sights but there was some resistance from the fans who referred to him as their 'jewel' in mid-field. He eventually left the club for Crystal Palace in October 1981 for a fee reputed to be around £200,000.

Houghton's assistant manager and coach at that time was a little known individual named Roy Hodgson who had joined Bristol City from Swedish club Halmstads BK. Like Houghton who had arrived at Bristol from Greek side Ethnikos Piraeus, Hodgson had felt it necessary to gain experience outside of the English League to actually get back in it. They had similar experiences with a similar outlook and when Houghton went, Hodgson took over as manager for a brief period in January 1982. He commented that his time at Bristol City was nothing short of a disaster. When he took over as manager he said that he was there simply to fulfil fixtures and oversee players leaving the club. It probably left a nasty taste in his mouth and he wanted to make sure he would not need to repeat the experience anytime soon.

The Roy Hodgson referred to is of course the current England manager (2015). He has commented on his spell as manager at Bristol using the following words taken from his Wikipedia file. It is assumed that these words reflect Hodgson's real feelings on the matter.

Bristol City was nothing short of a disaster in that we had only been there for a matter of weeks before the banks started to pull the rug from underneath the club. My job when I eventually took over, as caretaker manager, was quite simply to carry on in the aftermath of all the players leaving the club and just fulfilling the fixtures'

The boardroom battles would of course continue and with the best efforts of the new manager, the club slipped from Second Division to Fourth Division in the two years that Houghton was in charge and eventually he left in 1982.

CHAPTER ELEVEN

The Long and Winding Road

Leeds United had lost the services of Jimmy Armfield as manager and was now left with a board unhappy with the results they were getting. It was time for a change. It was 1979 when Jimmy left for a successful career in media opening the door for John (Jock) Stein, who lasted famously for 44 days before taking on the job as manager of Scotland. He had made a call to Tony Collins to see if he could get him and Maurice Lindley back together again, referring to them as the Morecambe and Wise of football. He wanted them to be part of his backroom staff and although it was usual for a new manager to bring his own staff with him, he would have been well pleased if he could have had this particular pair. Fortunately it wasn't to be, especially as Jock was only there for just 44 days before being replaced with Jimmy Adamson who in turn lasted until Allan Clarke (still referred to as 'sniffer' by those in the game) took over on September 16th, 1980. His assistant manager was Martin Wilkinson who, when the collapse of Leeds finally came in the June of 1982, would join Peterborough United for a short spell as Manager. Clarke also brought with him coach Barry Murphy who would also leave in the summer of '82.

Whatever rumours were floating around in Bristol, ace sports reporter Peter Godsiff had his finger on the pulse with an article headlined: *'Collins tipped for return to Leeds'*. In it he quoted both Clarke and Collins adding fuel to an already fiery boardroom situation at Ashton gate. It started with: *'Bristol City's assistant manager Tony Collins was today widely tipped to return to Leeds United as chief scout'*.

Tony stated that he: *'... didn't know anything about it, but it is flattering to hear that you are wanted.'*

On the date the article was released, Tony was officially joint caretaker manager at Bristol with chief coach Ken Wimshurst. Allan Clarke's comment was: *'It would be unfair at this stage to comment on the speculation about Mr Collin's return.'*

Tony, now a 54 year old, knew his new 'boss' well from Clarke's playing days at Leeds and there was a job to be done to try and arrest the general decline in Leeds United's performance on the pitch. The press greeted Tony Collins return to Leeds United with some degree of anticipation. The headlines of the day read: *'Talent-finder Collins is man for the job'* and *'The Commuter comes home.'*

Reporter John Wray noted at the time: *'Allan Clarke has yet to make his first player signing for Leeds United, but he made a potentially more important capture when he persuaded Tony Collins to return as chief scout.'*

So, the news at Elland Road was considered good with a manager and chief scout up for the battle to revive an ageing squad and stop the slow decline in performance that was seeing the once great Leeds team slip slowly down the division. In the 1980-81 season Leeds would finish 9th in the First Division, but no-one dare think the unthinkable that in the following 1981-82 season the once great Leeds United would languish at the bottom in 20th and be relegated to the Second Division. Times were tough – and going to get tougher, as revealed by Tony Collins in an interview with the Leeds United *Focus Magazine*.

'Football is currently facing recession that has nothing to do with the country's economic problems. That's the firm belief of United chief scout Tony Collins who returned to Elland Road in October for his second spell at Leeds after five years as assistant manager at Bristol City. Tony, respected as one of the game's leading talent spotters explains: 'The competition between clubs for good young players is as fierce as it has ever been. And the reason for that is because the general standard in the game has dropped in the last few seasons. The game is in recession at the moment with a scarcity of good players and if you look back over the years you tend to get these barren periods. It's not only the game in this country but also abroad. Take Holland as an example. To my knowledge the Dutch have not produced a World class player since Cruyff and Krol and it's a reflection on their shortage that they have even had to consider bringing back Cruyff into the national side'

No matter what state the game was perceived to be in, Clarke and Collins had their work cut out in 1981 and desperately needed players. The only significant signing of that year was the buy-back of Frank Gray, brother of Eddie Gray, purchased from Nottingham Forest for £300,000. The original sale value of Gray in 1979 was £500,000 so Tony considered this to be a good deal. This stalwart player would eventually make 396 appearances for Leeds and score 35 goals. Alex Sabella would return to his home in Argentina where he would play for Estudiente. The deal for the Argentinian would be struck at £120,000 and Jeff Chandler would also take a trip to Bolton Wanderers for around £40,000. However, the Leeds defence was desperately lacking and in an attempt to bolster it up, Kenny Burns was purchased from Nottingham Forest for around £400,000.

It was a see-saw set of results that witnessed the team sink inevitably to the bottom. Leeds, now strapped for cash, took on an exchange deal with Byron Stevenson for Frank Worthington from Birmingham City. He did make a difference, producing nine goals that season, but with the new three points for a win rule in operation there were some strong teams such as Sunderland and Stoke City all sitting on 44 points. Lady luck deserted Leeds United that year and so they were finally relegated.

However, in the midst of all of Leeds misfortunes, in the October of 1981 it was decided that for 'financial' reasons, some of the backroom staff would have to go. Maurice Lindley, Tony Collins and Bob English received their marching orders. Lindley was 65 and possibly expecting it but to Collins, it was something of a blow. The press at the time described the move as being the severing of the final backroom link with the Don Revie era at Elland Road, and that was perhaps much nearer the truth. Clarke's view was that unfortunately there was no alternative. The economics of the game at the time left him with no choice. The first notification letter from General Manager Keith Archer dated October 28th was short and sweet.

Dear Mr Collins,

I refer to the conversation between you and Mr Clarke on Wednesday 21st October 1981, when we informed you that it is unfortunately necessary for us to terminate your employment by reason of redundancy. We are prepared to pay you a settlement sum of £...... which will be tax free. Upon hearing from you that such a settlement is agreed, we will attend to the closing formalities.

From Tony's point of view there would be no agreement to such a settlement and so things became nasty with Mr Archer writing to Tony yet again on November 10th. However, this time it would be equally as short, but not quite so sweet!

Dear Mr Collins,

We refer to our earlier letter. We will regard your employment as being terminated with immediate effect and you will, of course, receive payment of your remuneration up to this date. Please make arrangements to return the motor car registration number RNW 556W with immediate effect. We shall be communicating with you again in the near future to arrange a meeting with you and your advisors regarding settlement.

At an employment tribunal on December 17th, an unhappy Mr Archer and Leeds United were required to settle the matter with a substantially increased severance amount and the car gifted to Tony as part of the final resolution. The said resolution carried with it a sort of 'non-disclosure' clause that the now redundant Mr Collins was asked to sign, and not wishing to extend the matter any further, he did so. Under the terms of this agreement Leeds United have been contacted by the authors on several occasions in an attempt to offer them an opportunity to comment on this situation without success. So that was the final date; the final outcome and by the end of 1981, Tony Collins had left Leeds United for the very last time … or had he?

Out of work and a bit out of sorts after the debacle with Leeds, Tony was unsure of what he really wanted to do next. He would have liked to find some gainful employment in the North near to his home base of Rochdale and his wife Edith. Sandra, the oldest child was now 27, Andrew 25 and Sarita 17. But things were moving in the First Division and Dave Sexton, the manager at Manchester United since 1977 had moved on to be replaced by Ron (Big Ron) Atkinson. His time at first

Division West Bromwich Albion had been marked by his joining of Brendon Batson with Laurie Cunningham and Cyrille Regis creating an unusual record in making 'West Brom' the first top division team to field three black players on a regular first team basis.

Big Ron was seen as possibly the only man who could add some 'pizzazz' to an already successful First Division team and in order to do that effectively, he would have to change the player line up. This would require the services of a scout, a damn good scout and so it was to begin all over again.

Detail of the deal was broken in the *Manchester Evening News* dated December 24th, 1981 by David Meek with the headline: *'Tony Collins United's new Chief Scout'*. He confirmed that Tony had indeed been signed by Ron Atkinson to replace Joe Brown who moved on to concentrate on bringing forward the youth team. He stated that for some reason or other, United had not been getting young players through the system. There was a lot to do and he felt that by bringing in Collins he would be able to divide some of his responsibilities. He commented:

'Tony is a real professional in this scouting business and is one of the most experienced in the game. I'm sure he will be a big help'

Len Noad of the *Sunday People* was surprised that there was *'precious little bally-hoo attached to the latest arrival at Old Trafford'*. He quoted Don Revie who had stated that Tony Collins was *'the best reader of a game in the business … and he's always prepared to back his judgement'*.

Len also noted that: *'The youngsters they picked up pre-Munich would have been worth millions today. Now Collins has to follow in the proud tradition laid down by Jimmy Murphy … a tough task from which he won't flinch'*

The 'pre-Munich' situation referred to by Len Noad was the unfortunate Munich air disaster which occurred on February 6th 1958 when the Manchester United team managed by Matt Busby and nicknamed in the press as the 'Busby Babes', were involved in a plane crash with many fatalities. The aircraft carrying the team back to Manchester after a European cup-tie with Red Star Belgrade, made several attempts to take off at Munich but failed to clear the runway. The resulting crash caused 23 deaths and 19 non-fatal injuries, decimating the young, fit and talented team Matt Busby had spent some years building. It was a personal tragedy for Busby, a crippling blow for Manchester United and a sad day for English football.

David Meek, the self proclaimed 'Voice of Football' heralded the arrival of Tony at 'ManU' with links back to Gordon McQueen and how he had been scouted for Leeds as a replacement for Jack Charlton. He reminded his readers that Collins was the one who engineered McQueen's move from St Mirran to Leeds for £35,000 and then sold him on to Manchester United for £500,000. Now Collins and McQueen were batting on the same side once more. When asked what the job of successful scouting really entailed, Tony answered:

> *'Scouting for me is like shopping is to a woman. You look in the window to see if there is anything you fancy, then you have to see how good a fit it will be with what you already have – and then you have to see how much you can get it for!'*

Ron had brought Bryan Robson with him from West Bromwich in October 1981 for a transfer record fee of £1.5 million and would stay with Manchester United after Ron Atkinson was rudely dismissed in November 1986. Robson was rumoured to have said that *'Money was not my main motivation. I simply wanted to be a winner'*. Following Robson to the new stable would be Remi Moses and Arsenal striker Frank

Stapleton. In 1982 he also gave an airing to a young near 17 year old Norman Whiteside. He would become the youngest player to appear in a World Cup event and the youngest to score in a League Cup and Cup Final. Being from Northern Ireland, Whiteside was constantly being compared with his fellow Irish soccer star George Best. However, he was quoted once as saying:

'The only thing I have in common with George Best is that we come from the same place, play for the same club and were discovered by the same man!'

Nothing to worry about there then!

With some well known and some not so well known names at Manchester United, the hunt was on to beef up the squad and one individual jumped to the top of the pile for Tony very quickly.

The signing of Paul McGrath came from an initial tip-off and to kick-start it all Tony received a call one day from Billy Beehan, one of his scouts in Ireland. He told him he had seen a very worthwhile young talent who played for St Patricks Athletic, a team struggling at the time to maintain momentum in the Irish league. Tony agreed to go over to Ireland to have a look. Even though the player came with a recommendation from Beehan, Tony knew it was important that the young lad could fit in with the existing players at Manchester United. So Tony flew into Dublin, and agreed he would meet Billy Beehan in the North Star Hotel. When Tony saw McGrath play he said it reminded him of Ruud Gullit in the way he got hold of the ball and laid it off. Whilst at the game Tony ran into Frank Carson, a well known comedian of the day, and they were both able to exchange views on the action. He had a chat with Billy after the match and arranged to see him in the morning before he flew back. Paul was signed to Manchester United and some would say he was one of the greatest players ever to come out of Ireland. He would make 63 appearances for United and score 12 goals. He would also become an International, playing 83 times for Ireland and scoring 8 goals.

In terms of beefing up the squad at that particular time it is interesting to note the story behind Peter Beardsley. So here is what actually happened with Beardsley, a talented Northumberland lad who found himself playing for the Vancouver Whitecaps after a few years at Carlisle United. He had made 104 appearances for Carlisle, scoring 22 goals, and 48 appearances for Vancouver, providing them with 20 goals. He moved to Canada when he felt it just wasn't possible to get a place with a first division team in England. With his ear close to the ground, Tony discovered, possibly through his agent, that the player would like to move back to the UK. Manchester United were on tour in Canada and Beardsley scored in a friendly against them – only 13 seconds after Ron Atkinson's side had kicked off! Beardsley was signed for £250,000, but his only appearance came in the League Cup. He rejoined Vancouver on a free transfer, but eventually Newcastle signed him for £150,000 in 1983 and he would go on to make 147 appearances for the team and score a useful 61 goals, pushing Newcastle into top flight football. The facts surrounding his purchase and then quick transfer from Old Trafford were that although Ron Atkinson and Tony Collins were very keen on him, the training staff who worked with him every day were not. They all liked his temperament and personality and he trained hard. However, they were all unanimous in claiming he was too small physically and ultimately the Manager and Chief Scout were outvoted, so he was allowed to leave. What a great opportunity for club and country was missed there then!

When Stevie Coppell received a bad injury, it was one that needed an operation ending up with Tony Collins taking the unfit player to a specialist hospital in Cambridge. As a result Tony, Mick Brown (Assistant Manager) and Ron Atkinson were considering some days later what they could do to replace him. Tony knew more than most about what was happening at Leeds United and also knew that a fine player named Arthur Graham (also a Scottish international) was playing in their reserves. The question had to be asked and so Tony asked it. 'Why don't we give Leeds a call and see if we can borrow him until the end of the season?' Mick Brown was unconvinced stating that Leeds were not going to let anyone 'borrow' an International player. So Tony countered with 'Well there's only one way to find out!' So the outcome was that they asked Leeds who did agree to lend him out and then finally in 1983, United signed him. Tony knew from his substantial contacts within the Leeds operation that they were struggling, and no one at Elland Road knew why Graham was not being played. However, as it happened, management were possibly keen to get him off the payroll.

Not all scouting trips for Tony Collins ended up with a signing. The story of Ruud Gullit is one typical example.

There were noises being made on the continent about a Dutch player named Ruud Gullit. Ron told Tony that rumour had it there was this terrific winger and centre forward at PSV Eindhoven, so Tony went off to Holland to see him. When Tony returned Ron asked him what he thought. Tony told him that Gullit was the best centre half on the field. Ron replied. 'You must be joking, you've got the wrong player, - he's no centre half!' Tony said 'Well ... you go and have a look, I'm telling you he was playing at centre half; he was brilliant — had the ball all the time!'

It turned out that Ruud Gullit could play in practically any position on the park with equal skill and they both thought he was a terrific player wishing they could have signed him. He was named player of the Year in 1986, and in 1987 Milan signed the brilliant all-rounder paying what was at the time a world record fee of £6m.

As the 1986-87 season came into play, the sparkle the Manchester United board of directors wanted had not materialised and there were rumours about the possibility of Ron Atkinson being 'moved on'. However, the scheming had actually begun on November 4th when Manchester United had been unceremoniously ejected from the Football League Cup. Chairman Martin Edwards, after seeing the clubs coffers recently revived by the sale of Mark Hughes to Barcelona for £2.3 million, felt confident and called a meeting next day of the other members of the four man board. Ron would have to go, the decision had been made. Who would replace him was the next big question and for some unknown reason, all four favoured the Aberdeen F.C. manager, Alex Ferguson. Allegedly, Ferguson received a phone call from director Michael Edelson who wanted to arrange a meeting between Ferguson and Edwards.

As a result of that arrangement, the four Manchester directors allegedly drove up to Scotland to meet the 45 year old Aberdeen manager, someone who had only managed Scottish teams in a short career from 1974 and the Scotland side for a brief period in 1985-86. A quick conversation with Aberdeen chairman Dick Donald and three days later, the deal was officially done – but not before the rumours started. As part of the substantial speculation surrounding the movements of Martin Edwards and journalistic guesswork, some names were being floated in the press and one of them inevitably had to be the ambitious Scottish League team manager, Alex Ferguson. He had been with Aberdeen since 1978 and now had itchy feet. His players had allegedly nicknamed him 'Furious Fergie' and the hard faced Glaswegian had set himself up with a reputation as one not to be messed with. However, he was destined to make his appearance as manger at Old Trafford on November 6th, 1986 after Ron Atkinson had turned up for training a few days before to find his boots had not been laid out. However, in their place there was a message to go and see the chairman.

Tony had had dealings with Ferguson before when the temperamental Scot was in charge at St Mirren and had therefore formed a view as to how long or short his own tenure would be as chief scout.

It started with unattributed comments in the press such as:

'United boss Alex Ferguson is busy overhauling Old Trafford's scouting network. He's unimpressed with a system that's thrown up only Norman Whiteside and Arthur Albiston for the current senior squad.'

He would produce a book titled *"Six Years at United"* and there would be some criticism of Tony Collins from what sounded like a slightly bitter Ferguson. He accused Collins of losing him John Barnes, costing him an extra £1.5 million to buy Gary Pallister and of being in charge of a sub-standard scouting operation. He stated that he might well have bought Pallister for £600,000 but that due to Tony's cautious attitude he later had to pay £2.3 million for the player.

Collins viewpoint was somewhat different and although Ferguson might claim he could have signed Gary Pallister for £600,000, Tony knew for a fact that such an aspiration was simply out of reach. He had already told Ferguson that Bruce Rioch and Colin Todd had built up Middlesbrough with a young team. He had put them on long contracts and said there was no way he would give either of them away … and he didn't!

Tony fought back against Ferguson's 'revelations' with a two page spread in the News of the World carrying an interview conducted quite carefully by Martin Leach. One of the quotes from Ferguson's book about Tony's lack of decision making brought up the situation with John Barnes who went to Liverpool when Ferguson was looking to sign him. He blamed the situation squarely on Collins.

However, from Tony's point of view the Barnes situation was not one of dalliance but of circumstances. He had made up his mind about Barnes when he saw him play for Watford at Rochdale. He had no worries about his ability but he really wanted some confirmation about his character, seeing what would happen to him playing on a wet and freezing night, on a soggy pitch sucking the strength out of a player at every move. Timing was also something to do with it, being just a month before Ron Atkinson was to be sacked; confirming the worst kept secret in English football. But despite that and on the basis of Tony's report, Ron, whilst still in charge at Old Trafford, arranged to have first option on Barnes. So, in effect, in terms of the club's responsibilities, the deal was actually done. Presumably, this was the point at which Ferguson, allegedly waiting in the sidelines for Ron to be removed, became aware of the situation. He had been told something, by somebody disconnected to the club staff, about Barnes and a low body temperature issue along with the fact he wore gloves in the winter. This allegedly had an effect on the decision to complete on him. So, being aware about Barnes contractual situation and not taking him up on an already agreed option was seen by Collins and his staff to be purely down to the indecision of Ferguson … not the chief scout!

Ferguson of course famously missed out on signing 'Gazza' but stops short of blaming that entirely on Collins. Tony had passed on a very early notice that Newcastle were going to sell Paul Gascoigne and during negotiations Paul confirmed the promise that he would sign for Manchester United. However, Alex Ferguson took his eye off the ball by deciding to go on holiday to Malta at that time and when he got back he found that 'Gazza' had signed for Tottenham Hotspur ... and it was a record fee of more than a couple of million.

Sports reporter Martin Leach made some observations about the row with Ferguson and his comments relating to John Barnes. He reminded his readers ... and Ferguson, that although the dour manager from north of the border was quick to write disparaging remarks about Collins in the Barnes situation, he was a little slow in coming forward with any form of praise for the work Tony did in capturing Lee Sharpe for Manchester. It was a manoeuvre masterminded by Collins and down to his first rate connections with the Torquay club management and board. Tony was originally tipped off about the 16 year old potential star by retired journalist Len Noad. Ferguson, Archie Knox, Collins and Noad slipped into a game with Colchester to watch the youngster. Knox was not so keen although Ferguson thought the lad was brave in play and had pace. Tony Collins pointed out to Knox and Ferguson that the Torquay manager Cyril Knowles had good connections with his old club Tottenham Hotspur and if they wanted Sharpe ... they would have to actually 'look sharp!' The deal was quickly done that night in some slightly unusual circumstances, and confirmed the next day with Cyril Knowles making the pertinent comment: 'I'm glad he's gone to a big club but, hand on heart, I would have liked him to join Tottenham!'

It was inevitable that Collins and Ferguson would not see eye to eye and the Manchester United boss wanted to desperately surround himself with his own people; people who thought like him, mostly acted like him and would 'tow the line'. Tony stated publicly that he was never comfortable with Ferguson. In fact, he found him cold and unresponsive. In his view, he felt Ron had easily taken on his shoulders and coped with the pressure of managing United. Ferguson however seemed to screw himself up with the responsibility and it soon became obvious that he appeared to be a man who would bear a grudge. Tony didn't think Ferguson had ever forgotten the fact he was with Bristol City when they beat his St Mirren team in the old Anglo-Scottish Cup. He also had a theory that over-caution, which Ferguson ascribed to Tony, could much better be exampled when someone spends £17 million on a team and then only plays one forward up front!

Tony's view of Ferguson was that he worked hard at being a 'Marmite' type of figure. You either loved ... or near worshipped him — or you hated him. Tony Collins neither worshipped him nor hated him but after working with him for several years, watching him perform as manager of a first class football club, he was left unimpressed and probably as a result ended up not liking him as a man. His ability to manage the technicalities of a team successfully would never be in doubt. However, many of the methods employed would be questioned by someone who had been at the blunt end of football as a player, manager and scout for over 45 years ... and Ferguson knew it!

So the day eventually came when Collins and Ferguson would have to 'part company' but not necessarily celebrated as an event of any significance. The letter from club secretary Ken Merrett dated August 2nd, 1988 was precise and to the point.

> *Dear Tony,*
>
> *I refer to our meeting on Thursday 21st July. In June of this year it was by mutual consent, orally agreed to extend your contract until the end of 1988. It is unfortunate the Club now have to terminate your employment. It only remains for me to thank you most sincerely for your service to the Club.*
>
> *Yours sincerely'*

Tony Collins walked away from Manchester United with no regrets.

He had done a job there, a job he was proud of despite the mumblings and grumblings of a completely self absorbed Alex Ferguson. It is strange to think that if Ferguson thought so little of Tony's talents, why did he keep him at United for over a year and a half after 'Big Ron' left the club. He had worked tirelessly for Ron Atkinson, a man he admired and who was dismissed in a most unacceptable manner. It did not go down well with many staff at Old Trafford and the rumours surrounding the possible replacement by Alex Ferguson had generally been seen as unwelcome. However, it was just about the wealthiest team in the game and with money can be purchased success, no matter how you spend it … as long as you spend enough, and Ferguson well knew how to do that.

At the age of 62, Tony had come to a crossroads in his life. Could he leave the game he had devoted literally all of his life to? As usual, he looked to Edith for counsel. Although the year of 1988 was more than half over there would be opportunity for someone like Tony out there as a new playing season was just about to start. For the family, a few months down the road all thoughts turned to the next big gathering at Christmas. Sandra by this time was married with two children and managing a hotel in Chester. Andrew had married Helen and Sarita was planning to go skiing on Boxing Day as she did every year at Christmas.

However, all was not well with Edith and on December 2nd 1988, she took ill with what everyone thought was simply a bad cold. This was the start of a deteriorating situation for the Matriarch of the Collins family and sadly on July 23rd, 1989 she passed away. The family were of course devastated and without his beloved Edith, Tony was left pondering on how his life would continue from that point forward. In 1985, Jim Smith had taken over as manager of Queens Park Rangers, a London club playing in the first division. After leaving Manchester, Jim invited Tony to join him at QPR as a scout. Jim was a fan of

European football styles and playing techniques and well aware of Tony's theories on field formations. The famous game against West Ham in August 1987 when Smith played the 3-5-2 formation resulted in a decisive win of 3–0 and caught the sporting headlines of the day. However, as soon as he arrived, Tony was on the move again with Smith who was to take charge at Newcastle United. He stayed with Smith until he left in the March of 1991. Ossie Ardiles, who took over from Jim Smith, was Argentinean and his real name was Osvaldo. He was a fan of the 4-4-2 formation and although he only lasted a year, Tony stayed with him as a scout.

In 1995, Jim Smith moved to Derby County and asked Tony to do some scouting work for him until Ian Broomfield became chief scout at Leeds United under David O'Leary in 1998. So – back at Leeds again for what he hoped would be a much calmer time with David and Ian. However, although things started out well, the 2001–02 season was put off course by a player incident in Leeds City Centre where an Asian student was assaulted and some Leeds players were involved. Chairman Peter Ridsdale was not happy with the adverse publicity for his team and even less happy with the contents of a book written by his manager, O'Leary, entitled 'Leeds United On Trial'. In the summer of 2002, David O'Leary left the club after discussions with Ridsdale and would eventually take up the reins at Aston Villa in June 2003.

Ian Broomfield would receive the call when O'Leary took the manager's job at Aston Villa and left Leeds to join him there. Tony Collins was pretty confident his time was now probably up and sure enough, when the new Chief Scout at Leeds was named as Adrian Heath he knew the 'letter' would be arriving very shortly – and it did. On July 9th, 2003, the new Chief Scout wrote the following.

'Dear Tony,

I write to inform you that I have recently been appointed as Chief Scout at Leeds United Football Club replacing Ian Broomfield who as you are probably aware has left the company to join Aston Villa. Consequently, following a review of the current staff and restructuring within the company, I regret to advise that your services are no longer required. Therefore, as per F.A. Premier League regulations, a Scout Cancellation Form has been forwarded to the F.A. Premier League to remove your details from our list of registered scouts thereby enabling you to seek alternative employment within the football industry.

In closing, may I take this opportunity on behalf of Leeds United Football Club to thank you for your assistance provided during last season whist working for our former Chief Scout, Ian Broomfield.

Yours Sincerely,

So, as Tony Collins knew all too well, good things must eventually come to an end and in July 2003 he left Leeds United for the final time at the age of 77. Ian Broomfield used to refer to Tony as his mentor so it was quite natural for him to look for Tony's services at Aston Villa. However, past injuries to hips and knees would eventually catch up with him creating problems in negotiating the steeply tiered steps at football grounds. So, it was now time for a new set of joints and reflection on what had been a great life generating a vast number of amusing episodes he had stored away to make him smile every now and again; something like the following.

Riding the 'Roller' coaster. During Collins tenure as manager at Rochdale, Eric Williams, who was a big pal of Freddie Ratcliffe the Chairman, would often come over to Rochdale from his home town of Conwy in north Wales, where he owned a holiday park. One day Rochdale were playing Sunderland away. It was an evening match and Eric asked Tony if he could go with him. Tony said, 'Sure, I'll meet you at the Craven Heiffer Inn near Skipton,' and confirmed a time. They met and after a quick chat, Eric who owned a rather nice Rolls Royce car said 'Let's take the roller!' so Tony agreed and as Eric, who really didn't like driving all that much, jumped in the passenger seat tossing the keys to Tony as he said ... 'You can work your passage!'

The team had gone ahead on a coach being booked to stay in a small hotel on the sea front in Sunderland. The team were just getting out of the coach when Tony and Eric pulled up outside in the Roller. Tony exited Eric's beautiful car with a casual 'Morning lads!' and walked casually into the hotel without further comment. Tony recalls the faces were a picture as he strolled away with shouts of 'Morning boss!' ringing in his ears. Perhaps they all thought that Tony Collins had won the pools ... or something!

A 'Cobbold' together story. There was of course much rivalry amongst managers and staff members in the game of football, but perhaps this little story may indicate that a sense of humour was a necessary requirement at all times. Each year all involved in professional football management would be invited to an annual dinner in a smart London venue somewhere or other. It would be a full-on dinner with some guest speakers and a great atmosphere generated by everyone attending more or less knowing one another. Tony recalls the events of one year, probably 1982 when he was scouting for Ron Atkinson and Manchester United. Both Alan Dicks and Bobby Robson were on the event management committee, and the directors of Ipswich Town, the Cobbold brothers, John and Patrick who owned Cobbold brewery, were there. They were staying over at the Royal Lancaster Hotel and on this particular evening, after the event, the brothers invited a few people up to their suite of rooms to carry on the party. The drinks were soon flowing and at one point the brothers had decided to relax and change into their pyjamas and smoking jackets. As the party became a bit louder and the conversation more animated, Tony, who was well known for his rather left field sense of humour, stood with his back to the door, and knocked on it as if someone was wanting to get in. So the Cobbold brother known by all his friends as Mr John said, 'Who the bloody hell is that at this time' and Tony replied with a straight face, 'I don't know Mr John, you'd best take a look'. He went to the door, opened it and seeing nobody immediately outside stepped out to investigate the corridor. Tony immediately closed the door firmly shut leaving 'Mr John' outside in the corridor of the rather posh Royal Lancaster Hotel in his pyjamas. Naturally the room full of rather inebriated gentlemen just fell about laughing as he hammered on the door for someone to let him in.

The 'Scottish' story. It was October 1975 and a reporter for the *Daily Record* with the by-line 'Sportsbag' made a startling and slightly embarrassing revelation that would haunt Tony for some months. The reporter revealed that an 'amazing document' had been discovered being what it described as a 'secret dossier' on the Scottish football team and predicting the result of the forthcoming match against England. The *Record* sportswriter Mr Gallagher had discovered the dossier which he said had been prepared for England manager Don Revie. The report highlighted Scotland's weaknesses following a game between Scotland and Wales and solicited what the newspaper called a 'remarkable response' from the Scottish football fans. Although Tony Collins has never admitted publicly to being the author of such a document, the press knew that only one person could put together such an accurate and unbiased view of a football match and the players within it. After the match that actually took place, the *Record* headline was 'Fans Back The Super Spy – Let's have our own expert' and the piece below stated that in their opinion 'England's Spy' Tony Collins of Leeds was right. In everything; his prediction of how the Wembley game would go and his summing up of Scotland's players. It went on to confirm that the report was clearly unbiased and showed up the faults of the Scotland team clearly. With a score line of 5-1 in favour of England, it appeared there was much to do in the Scottish camp to avoid such a humiliating defeat again. Admit it or not, just about all of the English sporting press knew the author was probably residing not a million miles away from Elland Road!

The 'Spanish' connection. Alan Dicks was a man who loved to travel. He would be happy to simply board any aeroplane and then ask where it was going. On one occasion recalled by Tony Collins, Bristol City were on a tour in Spain and arrived at the Andalucía Plaza in Marbella. Alan was in a great mood and he wanted a party. Unfortunately, he was not well known for his drinking capacity and soon fell by the wayside with Tony making sure he went to his bed. With the coach ready to leave early the next morning, all the players and staff had assembled in the foyer with the coach waiting outside. There was no sign of Alan, so Tony said he'd go and check his room. Unfortunately, when he arrived there Alan was still asleep lying sprawled on the bed with his trousers on. Tony woke him with a few choice words and helped him to dress and get his bag together. He eventually managed to steer him down to the waiting coach hoping that the state Alan appeared to be in was not too noticeable. However, it's not possible to get that kind of thing past a bunch of keen eyed lads, so both Alan and Tony were made to suffer the inevitable jeers and shouts such as; "Eh TC ... your mate doesn't look too clever does he?" Outside Tony had to play the disciplinarian and tell the players quite firmly that comments about the manager's condition were not welcome. Inside of course Tony was nearly overcome with laughter but couldn't let it show as he ordered the whole team on the coach, trying hard to maintain some acceptable level of authority.

~~~~

Now, having survived the biblical 'three score years and ten' by a considerable margin, Tony Collins knew it was a good time to take stock of a life that had been full of adventure, travel and sporting success along with the unswerving love and trust of an amazing woman and healthy family. But such a heavy sporting involvement had taken its toll on a body that now needed a few repairs. A replacement hip and knee was prescribed and it would take some considerable time for Tony to recover completely from such invasive surgery.

A few years later at the age of 80, he hung up his boots and driving gloves satisfied in the knowledge that whatever happened in the future, to the game he so passionately loved, he had done his best to promote the very best of it ... and some of the most well respected names within it. Tony Collins celebrated his 90th birthday on March 19th, 2016 with his friends and family around him along with some old 'mates' such as Tom Ritchie, Ian Broomfield and Gordon McQueen. He was at his happiest that day surrounded by people who had a passion for a game that has grown in England from an amateur 'kick-about' event to the highly professional sport it is today; awash with money and a weekly world audience of millions. Tony Collins played his quite substantial part in the successful growth of the 'beautiful game' by simply studying its science, the people who played it and the sometimes complex reasons for success and failure. Tony Collins; a man of opinions and determination, hailed by most in the game who knew him as ... the Master Spy!

CHAPTER TWELVE

Family

In all the hustle and bustle of a life measured by distances travelled, nights away from home and having a name constantly in the sporting headlines of most British National newspapers, it is sometimes difficult to remember that Tony Collins had a family. It was a very close-knit family and governed in no mean manner by the wonderful Edith. There was no doubt that Edith was the rock, the staunch supporter who provided a safe haven allowing Tony to pursue his career as the recognised Master Spy in the English game of football.

So, what was it like growing up in the sixties, seventies and eighties with a father who was rushing here and there and being something of a celebrity within the game of football? The best person to tell the story is someone who was part of it all. Tony's youngest daughter Sarita remembers those days very well and these are some of her own words.

'The good thing about being the youngest in the Collins household was that by the time I was six years old all the jobs in the house had been allocated. My sister Sandra was 16 and brother Andrew 14 and although I was never too sure what Sandra's jobs were, whatever she did was always accompanied by lots of raised voices, back chat and arguments over the beginning, the middle and the end.

Sandra was a strong character as a child and very much like her father which didn't always make for a quiet life. She was a confident, popular teenager and there were always more important things evolving in her world, outside the Collins household, than being tied into the perfect completion of chores and adherence to household rules. There was of course, the precious phone. It's probably difficult to understand now in a high-tech 2015, but our house was one of the few in the area to have a landline and whilst all our friends were traipsing back and forth to the phone box at the end of the street to make calls, we could use the telephone right there in the comfort of our own lounge. This heavenly situation however applied to the resident gossip hungry teenagers only when Tony was not in the house. When he was, of course, he was rarely off it with people phoning him not only from up and down the country but his many contacts in Europe as well. However, at the end of each month, the phone bill would need to be scrutinised by Tony as whichever club he was working for at the time paid for business calls only, and even in those days the bill was generally enormous. The use, or waiting for use of the telephone, was a major point of conflict in the homestead with Sandra nearly always expecting an incoming call about some 'very important' social arrangements and Tony either on the phone or expecting a call about some player deal or other. There would often be raised voices relating to such disputes with Sandra eventually stamping noisily up the stairs, slamming doors and issuing words of warning to a small sister if she happened to be hanging around the shared bedroom when a frustrated and hard done by Sandra entered.'

The telephone was very important in the life of Tony Collins but also a disruption to 'telly' addicted teenagers. It could be something like a Thursday night with 'Top of the Pops' in full swing. The phone would ring and Tony would instruct the Granada rented TV to be turned down. The phone would be answered and as feared it would be a football call — and an important one. So, everybody would be ushered, under great protest, out of the room.

'We always had to leave the room for dad's phone calls with none of us being sure if the subject matter was highly confidential or we were simply an unwanted distraction.'

Even Edith used to up sticks and go find some ironing to do or stitch a button on a shirt. There was always plenty of ironing to be done with a constant need of clean school shirts for the children and Tony wearing a suit and fresh shirt each day to go to work at the ground. Footballers of the time, much like now; were always up to speed with fashion and Tony, akin to the popular song of the period, was a 'dedicated follower' of it — as were his teenage children.

Sandra was unfortunately ill-equipped to end up becoming some sort of domestic goddess. In fact everything about her screamed 'party animal' and when she appeared at one, everybody there knew she had arrived. The Collins family was well known in the local area.

'We were all known by Christian name except me for some strange reason. I was mostly referred to as Sandra or Andrew's kid sister, or Tony Collins' daughter and rarely simply as Sarita.

This was probably because it appeared to be a strange sort of name for anyone to get their head round. I wish I had a pound for every time I was asked where that name actually came from, so to put the record straight, my mother had a naming baby book which gave the meaning of the name Sarita as the modern version of Sarah (Edith's mothers name) and thereby meaning 'little princess'. So to Edith, this seemed to be the obvious choice! I think the neighbours thought it was simply one foreign holiday on the Costas too many and they used to say to me 'is it Spanish?' thinking maybe perhaps I was really called Señorita!'

As Tony was spending more and more time away travelling to matches around the country, Sarita's brother Andrew became the stand in 'male' of the household and he was Edith's right hand man, especially when it came to her love of DIY or gardening. He would be sent on errands down to the garden centre at the bottom of the street for top soil, lawn tidy, a packet of seeds, a new rake, or round to Derek Addy's, the local hardware shop, for nails, maybe a hammer, some glue or shoe polish. Edith was quite happy most of the time when Tony worked for Bristol City. He had to go down to Ashton Gate for two or three days a week and regularly stayed at the Holiday Inn where he was very well looked after by the manager of the day, Horst Berl. Mr Collins was, without doubt, becoming one of the hotel's best customers!

Whilst the cat is away ... the mice will play and as far as Edith was concerned, the house would be fashioned just how Edith would like it. Tony didn't have time for any 'DIY' adventures or household repairs and would sooner have paid a tradesman to come in and make whatever changes Edith desired. However, Edith had different ideas knowing she had two hands just as good as anyone else's and a vision of what needed to be done. So, she could do it herself. Firstly, the fireplaces in the bedrooms were no longer needed as Edith had had central heating fitted, and they were now just an unnecessarily draughty hole in the wall. Tony went off to Bristol on one particular visit and by the time he returned, some three days later, the chimney breast in the main bedroom had been bricked up and papered! On subsequent trips the chimney breasts were all eventually bricked up by a satisfied Edith and her right hand man.

To Edith's delight, MFI, a new national furniture store chain, opened a branch in Rochdale and before the doors were fully opened, they had a new fan. Mrs Collins was either going to buy all their modern furniture ideas or make her own version of them, roping in a reluctant Andrew to help. Built-in wardrobes began to appear; sliding doors in one section and hinged doors on the other, along with shelving for shoes and lots of hanging space all built by a tireless Edith, who was also becoming an accomplished decorator. New gadgets began to appear in the kitchen and although there was a launderette just across the road a state of the art twin tub washing machine arrived one day, leaving the only thing the Collins kids needing to do was nip over and use the dryers. From Edith's point of view, as soon as you were old enough to cross the busy main road, you were old enough to do the laundrette run.

However, busy road or no busy road, there was an incident one day when Andrew, never one to refuse a dare, was tasked by his amused peers to lie down in the middle of the road to see how long he could last before being run over. One of the neighbours came round to give Edith the heads up!

'Mrs Collins – do you know your Andrew is lying down in middle of the road?'

Although everyone knew Tony had proven many times he could move at some pace down the wing, he would have had nothing that day on a furious Edith who was out in a flash. Unfortunately Andrew, who was having a nice relax in the middle of the road to amuse his friends, found he was soon to get his legs slapped as he was chased up the stairs to his bedroom. It has to be said it was difficult bringing up a boisterous young family, literally on her own, but Edith never backed away from the task being head chef, bottle washer and disciplinarian in the absence of her husband.

The Collins kids didn't worry too much about living on a busy main road. Sandra for example could regularly be seen balancing like a tightrope walker on the railings at the side of the pavement, until she fell one day and broke her arm putting an end to her tightrope walking career.

With Tony away, as he regularly was, Edith was left on her own to organise a birthday party at the house for Andrew.

'As I remember, it was possibly his ninth or tenth birthday and the month was July, so a nice summer party in the garden was planned with some games and sandwiches etc. Next door neighbour Yvonne would have me, the baby Sarita to look after, and so the friends arrived with their presents for Andrew and games were organised in the garden.

When they were finished there was a lull in the proceedings whilst waiting for parents to come and collect their little darlings. Mrs Collins, who was dressed up to the nines, in high heels, like one did in those days, looked very smart and composed as she said to the 8 or 9 fidgeting boys now beginning to look slightly bored:

'Well boys what would you like to play next?'

'Let's play fighting Mrs Collins' ... one shouted out, and without further ado, they all descended on her! Edith didn't look quite as glam and composed as she had planned to be when the parents arrived to collect their children. However, all the kids were saying what a great party it had been with a *'Thank you for having me'* offered in the direction of a dishevelled Mrs Collins who looked like she'd been dragged through a hedge backwards.' There was to be an eight year gap before the next party held in the garden. It was for Sarita's ninth birthday and a much less rowdy affair. On this occasion Edith was planning to impress

everyone with her daughter's birthday present; a full size table tennis table erected out in the garden. It actually was a 'Wow' moment with everyone taking their turn to knock a ball about. The best part of the plan for Edith was at the end of the summer and before the rain really set in, she would lay claim to what had now become her pasting tables before they warped in the rain. From then on, the table would be used for pasting up wallpaper with the table tennis novelty now having worn off.

The Collins kids could all be considered sporty. Sandra was quite athletic, but lacked the competitive spirit her father would have liked to have seen. With Tony watching one particular sports day at Green Hill School, in one of the middle distance running races, Sandra was leading by a good measure. In fact she was way out in front, but she slowed down and eventually stopped to wait for her friend to catch up. She would obviously never go on to partake in sport at a competitive level, but as she was considered fashionable and trendy and very vivacious she was encouraged to take part in local beauty contests, becoming 'Miss Courtaulds', beauty queen of the company she worked for. She also carried on working the 'beauty' circuit, collecting a few other local crowns along the way. Sandra had fortunately acquired some of her mother's dressmaking skills, and it wasn't unusual for her to get a length of fabric from Rochdale market on a Saturday afternoon and be wearing it, in some form or other, to go out dancing on a Saturday night. Even if the dress was only tacked together, she would still look stunning. There was no doubt Sandra was going to be a catch for some lucky, easy going young man — who hopefully could cook for himself!

Her boyfriends, and there were many, could mostly be considered good looking, generally self assured and quite sociable. They had to be; after all they were dating the daughter of Tony Collins, the local 'football man', who was on the payroll of Leeds United – currently the best team in the land.

Christmas Day was always fun in the Collins household. Everyone would be there who could get there. Grandma Murdoch (Edith's mother) and Aunt Rose (Rose Hodgson who with Arthur housed Edith and Tony during their time at York) would be there. Arthur by that time had passed away, so Tony and Edith insisted that Rose came to them for a few days over Christmas. To make enough room, Andrew and Sarita would sleep top to toe in the back bedroom with Sandra. Christmas Eve would require that Tony and Edith go up to The Crimble country club to see Freddie Ratcliffe who owned the place, and then be back for midnight. Tony would then turn into Father Christmas. Andrew, being 8 years older than Sarita, should have known better than wake her up to tell her quite loudly ... 'He's been!' He would then quickly beg Sarita to open 'just one' and eventually have her open the lot ... in the dark.

'In talking about Christmas, I have to say the Leeds United parties were something else with one of the players acting out a normally credible Father Christmas and dishing out awesome presents for the kids. One year I received an electric organ, a very expensive instrument of the day and the players would all put on a charity pantomime at the theatre in Leeds and we would always go and watch a simply hilarious performance. But unfortunately, all that joy and family feeling finished at Leeds when Don Revie left.'

Any New Year party at the Collins house would always stand out as being the place to be with up to fifty or sixty people turning up and many more dropping by. Sarita remembers that one year when Sandra was about 19, her boyfriend of the time, a young lad named Andy, had a bit too much to drink, and became a bit too loud. He was behaving generally very disrespectfully, and Sandra was becoming upset. Tony suggested Andy had had enough to drink and it would be a good idea if he left the party, but the lad wouldn't go, and said quite bravely 'Make me!' Tony Collins may have been in his late 50s at the time but was still very fit and so there was a bit of jostling. Still the lad would not leave and so punches began to fly, which resulted in Andy acquiring a broken nose. He returned a few days later to apologise for his behaviour and although the incident marked the end of a romance it didn't stop the party.

As an example of how Sarita's father inter-reacted with his family, one day Tony was having a kick about in the back garden with Andrew. Unfortunately, when Andrew kicked the ball at one particular point, it smashed straight through the dining room window. Edith ran out into the garden expecting Tony to be giving Andrew a verbal dressing down. She came out guns blazing shouting to Tony ... *'look what he's done!'*

Tony replied calmly; *"I know. I've told him he has to learn more control and strike the ball with his toe down and his heel up, or it will just go wildly up in the air ..."*

Edith was stunned. *'What! ... Is that all you've got to say about it?'*

Andrew took a step back with a bemused sideways glance at his father who was now firmly in the firing line for what had happened, and was getting the rollicking. Good old Tony!

He also had the last word *'Well Edith dear, he's got to learn.'*

There were the usual family arguments in the Collins house of course, but the buck always stopped with Tony. Andrew had made it clear that primarily he wanted to be a footballer and even enjoyed a spell of training with Leeds United. But it was not to be and when it came to leaving school, what else would he want to do if he couldn't be a footballer? He said he fancied working on the roads; doing something physical. Tony calmly advised his son that his body would probably be in tatters by the time he was 40, and therefore encouraged him to take a slightly less strenuous and possibly safer position with the Midland Bank. Andrew also wanted a motorbike, but with the experience Tony had gained, driving the length and breadth of the country witnessing many road accidents involving motorbikes, he told his son quite bluntly that if he acquired one, Tony himself would make sure it was smashed into pieces. That was it and as usual this would end up being the final word on the subject.

So, an un-phased and determined Andrew obtained a van instead, and never looked back as it became the 'mobile' element of his 'mobile disco'. He would become very successful with this sideline, and in due course when Sarita was 24 he trained her up as a DJ being the birth of a business that went on to specialise in children's parties, family parties and events up and down the country.

"We all say that whatever natural DJ'ing talent any of us have, we definitely get from mum. She used to orchestrate the playlist at all the family parties; she loved playing records, and the radio was always on whether at her shop or at home and Edith was always up to the minute on who was moving up and down the charts."

Back on the DIY note, one week TC was going to Bristol for a few days, leaving enough time for Edith to do a real project. So with Andrew's help Edith dug up the front lawn and moved it round to the back of the house. In the front, she laid some sort of crazy paving and when Tony arrived home a few days later he walked past the gate as he didn't recognise the garden. When he finally realised he had passed his own house he hit the roof. His words were something along the lines of *'It looks like a dog's toilet!'* although in reality, it wasn't all that bad.

However, on his next away trip mum and Andrew had to put it all back … just how it was.

Edith loved to decorate, but sometimes she would become a little too thorough. She once decided to wallpaper behind the floor-standing boiler, in an area that would never really have been seen, so on this particular day Edith got 'stuck into' the project with 'stuck' being the operative word. When Sarita returned home from school in the afternoon, she could see a bottom sticking out from the boiler area in the kitchen. It was an unexpected and obviously amusing sight and she began to laugh wondering what on earth mum was doing on her knees with her head under the boiler. A panicking Edith shouted out *Thank god you're home … help me, I'm stuck … I've been here for hours!'*

There was obvious panic in her voice as she had somehow jammed her head between the central heating pipes. Under Edith's directions she managed to prise the pipes just wide enough for her mother to retrieve her head. The real panic of course was that the central heating was due on at 4pm and the pipes would then have been very hot, in fact hot enough to have possibly scalded Edith's neck. That was a near one!

From the age of 11 or 12, on every birthday, Sarita had pestered mum and dad for a dog and each year she would be told that keeping an animal and living on a busy main road would eventually end in tears. There was the obviously high risk that if the dog escaped the confines of the house, then it may well be knocked down. Sarita kept receiving splendid presents for her birthday but what she really wanted was a dog. Eventually, with Sandra on her side, she persuaded Tony that he should at least look. So Sandra, dad, Sarita and a friend set off to the local kennels. Edith had issued an instruction to Tony not to come back with a dog and that they were simply 'not animal people!' Tony said not to worry as he wasn't really taking any money with him.

However, unbeknown to her father, Sandra did carry some cash and when they all arrived at the kennels they were asked if there was any breed we particularly liked. Sarita piped up 'Golden Retriever', so they were taken to see a male puppy sitting sadly on his own. It was love at first sight as he made a beeline for her. There was no way Tony was going to say no to both his daughters and he told them that their mum was going to kill him. Sandra said it wouldn't be that bad and she had the money with her, so the puppy was given the name Quest by Tony as he had previously had a dog called this, and now Quest was on his way to a new home and new life at 54 Edenfield Road.

Edith was definitely not happy, but the dog was very cute and her final comment was: *'As long as you don't expect me to have anything to do with him …!'* A few weeks later they were buddies but unfortunately he was a sickly puppy with an eyelid problem that made his eyes water. With that and a bout of suspected distemper, Quest became a regular visitor to the nearby vets.

Sarita remembers: 'I religiously fussed, brushed, walked and ran Quest taking him playing football with me on the school field. In fact, I took him everywhere with me. But I wasn't the only softie when it came to looking after Quest.'

Tony went off to Scotland to watch a match one day and the dog was poorly, finding it difficult to sleep. Tony arrived home that morning at 2am and was trying to comfort Quest on the living room floor when the exhausted dog fell asleep resting his head on TCs arm. For fear of disturbing him, Tony spent the whole night on the floor just so Quest could get some sleep! Edith of course 'gave him some stick' and told him he must be mad, but she was often just as bad. Sarita remembers one particular event whilst Tony was at Manchester United when he took an early finish on a Thursday afternoon, as there were not usually matches on a Thursday night. He would often use this free time to take Edith up to the Crimble for lunch. As a result, there would be no meal on the stove for Sarita when she returned home from work as they had both already eaten. But one Thursday she opened the door to find the house filled with a gorgeous smell of cooking. She enquired as to what was in the oven, to be told: *'It's Rabbit!'*

'Oh,' she said *'I've never had that before!'*

'Well it's not for you – it's for Quest – he's been off his food!'

Edith would maintain vehemently that she simply wasn't keen on dogs, however most evenings Quest would wriggle himself up onto Edith's arm chair and try and get behind her. Eventually of course, he would stretch his legs which would result in Edith sitting on the floor leaving Quest conked out in the arm chair! She could also be heard regularly chatting away to him in the garden and both Quest and Edith were keen on gardening in their own separate ways as he would dig the holes – and Edith would fill them in!

~~~~

In her early years as a child, Sarita didn't notice that her dad was black and her mum was white. To some, never having been in such a situation, it may seem a strange thing to say but it was only when she invited a friend back after school one day that they pointed it out to her. She hadn't really seen anyone else she could identify simply as a 'dad' so didn't really know that hers was different. She recalls that once on holiday, a guy came up to Tony in the supermarket and said without any particular malice; 'Cor, that's hell of a suntan you got there; what do you use?' So Tony told the man he used Olive Oil. A few days later, the family saw the same guy walking off the beach and he was lobster red. At the time of the enquiry, Sarita said that Tony hadn't known whether or not the man was trying to be funny, so had given him the answer he felt the enquiry deserved. Looking back on the incident and the time period, it's difficult to know if the question was meant to be cynical or not. What kind of reaction would such a question solicit from a dark skinned man today, and would the enquirer be labelled a racist? Edith had a natural sensitivity that made her commit to never seeing Tony play in front of a crowd in case he had a bad game and 'got stick'. This meant having to listen to possible racist comments ... that could be taken personally. However, perhaps that wasn't just peculiar to him as Sarita is pretty sure that not many players' wives went along to the games in those days.

Tony and Edith did however both go to watch some big games together and one rather memorable event was the 1975 European Cup Final in Paris. At first Edith didn't want to go, more through shyness than anything else. She felt that all the other girls, the player's wives, would be much younger but Tony eventually persuaded her. He was confident this could be a win for Leeds United and wanted her to be at his side on what should have been one of the greatest accolades in his career. So a reluctant Edith went with all the other wives making her very welcome. The women had a separate entertainment programme in Paris from the men and after enjoying a relaxing cruise on the Seine, the mood was positive excitement. However, after the result of the match spirits were significantly dampened.

In terms of family humour, Sarita remembers that her father had a rather unique knack of mimicking people and taking off accents. She heard that sometimes he would ring up other clubs to try and get some advance notice of the team-sheet, just to see which players would be in the playing squad so that if a particular player he wanted to watch wasn't in the team, then Tony wouldn't have a wasted journey.

Naturally, he wouldn't want those teams to know who was interested in their players, so for example, he would ring up putting on a strong West midlands accent, purporting to be calling on behalf of West Bromwich Albion.

~~~~

What do we know about family and the football connection? Was there one? Well Sarita remembers some of the excitement of it all as follows.

"When on one occasion we went to Wembley with Manchester United, we travelled by train with the wives and families of the players with everyone staying at the Royal Lancaster Hotel. The morning of the match a coach was laid on for us all to get to the ground. The coach dropped us off at the edge of Wembley Way and we had to walk the short distance to the steps and even though we arrived early, a substantial crowd was already building up. We were all very excited as we mounted the steps leading up to the turnstile when there was an unexpected surge from the crowd behind us.

Dad got hold of Mum and then attempted to push a way back down through the crowd to get to me. I could hear dad desperately shouting for us all to stick together. Unfortunately that was easier said than done with a sea of energised and determined people surrounding us. I managed to find a place tight up behind a policeman and together we literally surged up the steps, crowd surfing. It was of course very frightening for a teenager at the time, but I survived, breathless and waiting at the turnstile for mum and dad to now fight a way back up to me. I was left concerned as to how some of the other ladies would cope in a crowd like that.

When I went to most football matches, I would be fortunate enough to find a welcome in the director's lounge and box. I always dressed up to go to football. Whereas most people would normally dress down or go in jeans I was used to being introduced to lots of what I considered to be 'important – well known' people in the football business. I would often sit next to Harry McShane, ex-Manchester United player, father of the well known actor Iain McShane and Joe Glanville, head of the Maltese supporters club. Mum and Dad were very kindly invited by Joe for a holiday in Malta, and they loved every minute of it."

For someone totally absorbed by the game such as Sarita, it was a great thrill being able to accompany her father who had the freedom to walk into practically any director's box at any club ground in the country. This of course was an unusual privilege, and one that has left her with poignant memories.

17 — Rochdale Club staff dinner at The Crimble

18 — Bristol City squad

19 — Tony and Edith at a Torquay club dinner event

20 — Quest   21 — Alan Dicks   22 — Edith

23 — A Butlins Trip   24 — Testimonial   25 — A day at the Office

26 — Tony with Freddie Ratcliffe

27 — Tony with Edith and FA Cup

28 —   Manchester United Team —   1987

29 — Don Revie ... a gathering of
friends near the end

30 — Tony with Jimmy Hill &
Nat Lofthouse

31 — Tony Collins with Gerry Gow 2011

32 — Tony Collins 2011

PART THREE

What I Thought of Them All

CHAPTER THIRTEEN

Edith and Beyond

There had to be one singular driving force in the story of a man who rose to particular success in a sport where normally once your 'kicking' days are over, there is little left to consider in terms of a continuing career. A life spent travelling around 40,000 miles a year by car, year in – year out and probably several times that amount on aeroplanes requires some strong household management, especially with three boisterous children to look after. A safe haven to come home to, no matter what happened in the workplace, was the centre point of Tony's success. Edith was of course that centre point; an immovable anchor firmly established at 54 Edenfield Road, Rochdale.

Preparations for another family Christmas were at the forefront of Edith's mind when the December of 1988 came around. She felt hard pressed and perhaps a little 'under the weather', and on the second of the month she took quite ill with what all reckoned was a bad cold. It was in fact so energy sapping that Edith was forced to take to her bed for a few days. It left her feeling quite tired and experiencing problems taking deep breaths.

The doctor was called and diagnosed an amount of fluid on the lung, a problem which was quickly rectified with a painful but effective treatment to extract it with the aid of a fine needle. As a safeguard, the doctor stated he would send the fluid off to 'the lab' for a biopsy report ... just a precaution of course. Edith was relieved; she felt much better and now wanted to catch up in order to prepare for the forthcoming celebrations. However, advice from the family was that Edith needed some more recovery time before taking on such a task and so alternative arrangements would have to be made. Her eldest daughter Sandra was now a 34 year old; someone who had just about survived her teenage years unscathed and was happily married with two children and one more on the way. She and her husband successfully managed a hotel in Chester. Edith's son Andrew at the age of 32, was also married leaving only 24 year old Sarita at home continuing to work at the local bank, but with ambitions to move on to better things.

The decision was made for the whole family to travel to Sandra's property for the Christmas celebrations. Edith was simply not up to hosting a house full and with the hotel closed and therefore empty over the holiday, there was room for everyone. Needless to say, the Collins family had a great time with Edith enjoying every moment in close contact with her grandchildren Bianca and Carlene. Andrew was there with his wife Helen and Sarita, who normally went skiing on Boxing Day, had made arrangements to leave early and fly off to the Italian Alps.

The bad news arrived shortly after Sarita returned home on January 3rd 1989. It stopped everyone in their tracks. The result of the biopsy was not what anyone was expecting ... least of all Edith. What had been considered to be a bad chest infection by just about everyone was in reality advanced signs of lung cancer. It was in fact a secondary condition to ovarian cancer which had developed unnoticed. The family were devastated but all were of one opinion in that they all knew Edith was a fighter and if anyone could tackle the situation head-on ...

it would be her. Sarita made a decision to give up her job at the bank and look for a more absorbing career working for herself whilst devoting time to care for her mother and look after her father. These are some of her own recollections of the time:

'Mum and I were extremely close as we had spent quite a few years together; just the two of us. When dad was away at matches we would spend many hours, on our own, and we could tell one another just about anything. We were both very calm and hopefully quite practical in discussing what we could do to help the fight, looking at nutrition in particular and anything we felt would make a difference.'

Edith was scheduled to attend the Christie Hospital in Manchester and whenever she and Tony needed to visit, Sarita would make sure she was also with them, asking probing questions, attempting to cut through the medical jargon of the day and get to the heart of what real and effective treatments were available. It was probably due to this intensive questioning that the consultant agreed to put Edith on a new trial drug based on interleukin research and immunotherapy treatment.

All seemed to be going well from January to March with regular blood counts showing some improvement and with little or no associated sickness as expected, the Collins family were confident that perhaps Edith was on the mend.

In the meantime, Sarita was preparing for her new venture as a business owner and had decided that the world of child development, in the form of a children's physical play and education franchise was the right road to go down. Juggling her responsibilities between looking after her parents and setting up her new business, Sarita had a lot on her mind. Transport had to be found, stock purchased and staff interviewed as well as some fairly intensive training undertaken in distant Nottingham. The first two centres were due to open in April and around that time Edith's consultants decided to change her medication as they felt that not enough progress was being made.

That appeared to be a turning point for someone who had fought so hard to beat her condition, bury the pain and stay remarkably positive. As a result Edith became uncomfortable and nauseous as well as finding food difficult to digest. All the signs were there and during the second week of April, Sarita's mother went to stay for a few days at the Christie Hospital for some close observation. The business was in launch phase and the two franchise owners had travelled to meet with Sarita and provide support along with a little more staff training for her two new outlets. The first one was at a hall in Rochdale and when Sarita received the message from her brother Andrew that Edith had taken a turn for the worse, she literally dropped everything and set off for Manchester. She left a note for the franchise owners, Bill and Jenny Cosgrove advising what had happened and that the keys for the van containing all of the play equipment, were in fact in the garage across the road from the venue. This message was never received and whilst Andrew was driving Sarita and their father to the hospital, the Cosgrove's were left to provide a slightly restricted service to Sarita's new customers. She remembers the situation as follows:

'It was difficult knowing what to say to my mum except to tell her she had been the very, very best mum any person could wish for. She was semi conscious by the time we arrived at the Christie and I whispered in her ear not to be afraid and to give my love to grandma in heaven. I was convinced we were losing her and this massive deterioration in her condition was sudden and unexpected. After talking with the doctors and staff, and a long time waiting for an indication as to what was eventually to happen, by some form of near miracle, mum began to recover slightly and then eventually regained consciousness. Some days later, she had improved enough to be allowed home and I promised to look after her and provide everything that was necessary. It was a relief to us all.'

The whole family were in good spirits as Edith arrived home and although weak and still very unwell, there appeared to be much to hope for. Sarita limited her new business activity to two days a week so that full time care could be organised for her mother.

This was of course a hectic time for Edith's youngest daughter, spending much time upstairs having chats with her mother and then downstairs, keeping Tony company ... when he was home between matches. Sarita recalls when her mother's friend Hazel Siddall came to visit and the three of them were in Edith's bedroom watching the Hillsborough disaster unfold on television. Hazel commented on the fact that people were running on to the pitch, branding them as hooligans. Sarita and her mum however saw people throwing themselves off the stands and upper tiers and others hanging on by their fingertips. It was a sobering moment in what had been a day looked forward to by Edith.

~~~~

As the weeks went by there was unfortunately little improvement in Edith's condition. Spring had turned into summer and the warmer days of June would allow Edith to spend some time out of doors in the garden she loved so much. Sarita remembers one particular occasion.

'I was in the garden with mum one day and she told me that when she was probably semi-conscious in the hospital, she could hear our voices but felt as if she was somehow trapped in a tunnel and being drawn to a bright light at the very end. She said that part of her wanted to go there, right to the very end, but somehow the sounds of our voices were drawing her back. She also told me she heard what I had told her about seeing grandma and thought it to be very sweet.'

Typical of Edith of course was her unselfish thought for others. One day, when she appeared to be a little brighter than usual, Edith suggested to Sarita that Tony should invite Judith Ratcliffe down to the house to keep him company. Judith was Freddie Ratcliffe's daughter and a keen football fan. They had much in common with their love of football.

Sarita's feelings at the time were that Edith was making some attempt to find someone to look after Tony if she didn't make it. She knew well that Tony was not the most efficient of housekeepers and his whole adult life had been one spent under the watchful eye of Edith who had looked after him and cared for him to the point he had simply nothing to worry about on a day to day basis but football! He was untrained in the finer arts of cooking, washing and ironing and a vacuum was a strange and rather noisy electrical item normally resting out of sight in a cupboard. There was another reason of course in that Edith wanted Sarita, her youngest daughter, to have her own life in the event that she passed away and not be bound to Edenfield Road and the needs of her father. Sarita's mother knew her well and wanted her to have her own life.

'My mum knew me so well. I remember that at about 5 or 6 years of age she wrote in a photo album she feared that 'Sarita' was much too sensitive for this world!'

On July 11th, Sandra gave birth to her third child, a beautiful little girl named Rochelle. She brought the baby to Edenfield Road for Edith to see and this was an outstandingly lovely moment for the whole family.

However, dark clouds were gathering and some days later Edith went back to Christies and when the family were all called on July 23rd, they knew that this time it really would be the end. The surgical team had done their best to remove an advancing tumour and although the actual operation itself had gone well, Edith's recovery had not. She had gone into shock after the necessary operation and it was particularly distressing for all the family to see her wrapped in a foil blanket looking quite lifeless. There was no way this courageous fighting spirit could battle on much longer.

All were assured that Edith could hear what was being said but unable to respond in any particular manner. One by one, every member of the family said goodbye, and everyone promised at her bedside that there would be no worry about Tony as the children, their children, Sandra, Andrew and Sarita would make sure he was well looked after. Sarita recalls how she reacted to her mother's passing:

'Again, I remember being very together at the time in terms of communicating with hospital staff and resolving possible donor issues. I even drove everyone home; but when we arrived I discovered my new business van had been broken into and vandalised. In the general shape of things, it was nothing really, but unfortunately it was probably the 'straw that broke the camel's back' and it set me off on the road to tears ... a state I would remain in on and off for some days. Dad was the same and we would spend our time sitting together ... endless hours, drinking Port and both wondering how life would carry on without our rock, our strength ... our Edith!'

Both Sarita and Tony knew they would have to stay strong for each other. There was a funeral to plan, people to talk to, lives to be organised and memories to share with pride.

The funeral was remembered by Sarita as a nice affair, as far as funerals go of course. Many people turned up to pay their respects and support Tony including Billy Bremner and lots of other football related friends along with many locals and friends of the children. A chapter, a very long and accomplished chapter in everyone's life had ended and now it was time to look to the future. Tony was still employed and had continued to stay in contact with his work throughout Edith's illness. After her passing however, Sarita and her father were more or less 'thrown together' to use Sarita's words; now being the sole residents of a very empty feeling 54 Edenfield Road.

'So, dad and I were sort of 'thrown together' by simply living in the same house. I don't think either of us could cook much and as most mothers did in the seventies, I was allowed to watch her and help a little in the kitchen but mum could be quite territorial. The kitchen was 'her' place, a space where she was fully in charge. Dad could not competently boil water and when mum had the bed and breakfast business in Torquay she asked him one morning to watch the toast whilst she took some breakfast orders. With the smell of burning in the air, Edith rushed back to the kitchen to find the toast on fire. She asked Tony why he didn't remove the toast from the grill when he saw it burning. He replied slightly distressed that she had only asked him to watch it!'

Sarita knew well that Tony would be as lost as she was without Edith who had related to Sarita when she was much younger how Tony would follow her around the house when he wasn't playing. He simply wanted to be with her and his whole mindset was to make sure that Edith was ... OK!

Before her passing, a cruise had been planned by Edith and Tony to celebrate their 40th wedding anniversary, but that of course was not to be. The point at which Tony would leave football behind him had also been discussed and it was agreed they would eventually retire peacefully to their beloved Cornwall. However all these plans were now empty of substance but played on Tony's mind for some considerable time.

Sarita also reminisced about her time together with her mum and dad. She remembers she was quite shy as a young girl and not that confident around boys.

'The three of us, mum and dad and I, would go on holidays every year together to the Watergate Bay Hotel in Cornwall. We were the gang of three; we were a team and always had a ball lurking somewhere in the day's hand baggage which we would kick about. I would play all the sports on offer including squash, badminton, tennis, and snooker. The hotel would hold competitions and many a comment would be made about 'that girl and her father' playing snooker and kicking a football around. Mum and I would regularly go into Newquay to spend wonderful days together with dad dropping us off in town and retrieving us later.'

Looking back, Sarita knew that such experiences were her building blocks and would stand her in good stead for perhaps some difficult days to come.

'They were days when we all felt very connected and there didn't appear to be any times of awkwardness that some young girls experience going on holiday with their parents.'

Now the 'team' was down to two and the fantastic family dog, Quest. He would receive extra long walks during the healing process, sometimes with Sarita and Tony and others with Sarita on her own. These walks were no doubt therapeutic, allowing them to both be out and about amongst their neighbours and friends who all talked so well of Edith.

Tony made the decision to work mainly part-time enabling him to spend a bit more time at home. Sarita was focused on building her business but between them a new, comfortable routine soon developed. Like a long distance runner, once you stop or slow down, the physical pain of it all begins ... and that was what happened to Tony. A knee replacement became essential to keep him mobile and recovery would turn out to be a long winded affair. The loss of Edith still haunted day to day life at Edenfield Road but as the months passed, both Tony and Sarita learned to cope in their own way using each other for support.

Judith Ratcliffe, who had remained a good friend to both Tony and Sarita, came round to visit regularly. She would often come to the house to look after Quest on a Saturday when Tony was at a football match and Sarita was working her party business now named as Fun Unlimited. A best quality steak would often appear as Tony returned home and Judith would cook it for the both of them. They were good 'pals' and had a common interest in all things football, which perhaps took the sting out of the much feared feelings of loneliness experienced when you lose a partner of nearly 40 years.

~~~~

Some fourteen years would pass before any major change would take place in the routines of day to day life for Tony Collins. Quest would eventually leave the family creating much sadness until Will, the new golden retriever, came along. It was a time of reflection for Sarita, someone who was passing through the time when having children may have been a real possibility. Moving out would have allowed her a greater level of independence of course but it would also mean there would be two houses to clean ... rather than one. So, not looking for a particular future with anyone else, she had more or less resigned herself to the continuing home partnership of her father, and Will the dog.

There was one period of a few years when Sarita had found herself embroiled in what she thought could turn out to be a long term relationship. However, it eventually would lead to nowhere in particular until in 2004 her current partner William came on the scene. The tough choice had to finally be made when Sarita moved out of the house leaving Tony and Will together. Although the decision may have appeared selfish at the time, everyone with a sensible opinion knew it was the right and natural thing to do. Sarita, despite a busy business life, would continue to look after her father in every way possible, as she still does today (2015) ... and as promised to her mother.

CHAPTER FOURTEEN

Some Names You May Know

Norman Hunter: One question regularly asked in football circles of the time was how Norman Hunter eventually ended up at Bristol City. The truth of the matter was that Collins, knowing well what was happening at Leeds in relation to the building of a new, younger and more aggressive team, also knew that some of the old guard would soon be going and Hunter would be top of everyone's wish list. Collins wanted to get in first and rang Norman Hunter to test the temperature of the water.

'How's things Norm?' Tony asked.

'Well you know how it is Tone,' he replied 'not the same as it was!'

'Why don't you come with us? We've got a good young team and one that would benefit from your experience. Have a think about it and let me know.'

Norman did have some reservations about moving his family down to Bristol but eventually agreed to a discussion, allowing Tony to arrange a meeting with Alan Dicks. The rest, as they say, is history except for needing to pass the move by the board at Bristol. One director, whose name Tony had forgotten, was reluctant and said so. Tony told him directly:

'So ... you don't want Hunter? Well, I can tell you there are quite a few people who do … and you had better make your mind up!' The unnamed director gave in and the transfer went ahead as planned. The signing of Hunter, someone who had won 'Player of the Year' award in 1974, was completed by Bristol for a figure of around £40,000 on 28th October, 1976. He stayed until 1979 after making over a hundred appearances for Bristol and left for Barnsley where he played and eventually became manager in 1980. Tony and Alan Dicks got on very well with 'Bite Yer Legs' Norman, known as the 'hard man' of Leeds United. Both agreed he played a major part in stabilising the young Bristol team at just the right time from joining the first division in 1977 up to winning the Anglo Scottish Cup in the 1977/78 season. As previously noted, that was achieved of course by beating a young, inexperienced Alex Ferguson's St Mirren.

~~~~

Bill Shankley: Here was a man considered famous to many and possibly infamous to some, but he was someone admired by Tony Collins and they had first met when Tony was playing in a reserves match for Sheffield Wednesday. They were competing against Preston North End reserves, and Tony found himself playing directly opposite a young Bill Shankley. Even at that stage in his short but impressive football playing career, Shankley was known on the field as a hard player. Tony of course was just a youngster but felt he had a reasonable game against the more experienced Shankley, whose brother Bob also played for Preston. Some years later when Tony had arrived in the rather hectic world of football management and necessarily gaining entrance into various club boardrooms around the country, their paths would cross again. As soon as Shankley met Tony for the first time off the pitch, he pointed at him and calmly stated 'Tony Collins – Sheffield

Wednesday!' Shankley was a quite amazing personality and a man that prided himself on never forgetting a face. Tony was slightly taken aback, wondering how on earth Shankley, the revered manager of Liverpool, had remembered him. Initially, showing the correct level of respect for such a well known figure, Tony addressed him as Mr. Shankley until he was told quite casually to call him Bill. Collins recalls that once someone was 'in' with him he would introduce you to his circle of friends and this level of contact, along with the ability to be recognised in such established circles, would turn out to be invaluable to the young Rochdale manager. Bill Shankley used to have a space just off the boardroom at Anfield called the 'Boot Room' and Tony was proud to be invited to this inner sanctum by Bill who always made him welcome there. The room was equipped with a bar where Tony would be offered a drink so the two of them could sit and chat about their all absorbing interests in the game of football.

Tony was always guaranteed a warm reception at Anfield and unrestricted entrance to the director's lounge. If Shankley saw him there he would make a beeline for him and in his strong Scottish accent would enquire as to Tony's health and what he would like to drink. He would then invariably want to take Tony off somewhere for a quiet chat ... about football of course. It was in one of these conversations that the subject of Norman Hunter came up and the story behind Tony's part in signing him for Bristol City. Tony agreed that he was a type of player that would suit Bill. His reply was 'Aye son, you can't buy Hunter's these days!' Shankley was well known in the game for being able to sum up the character of an individual at 20 paces by their body language. He was no student of the science but held on to an innate skill, probably developed through his hard upbringing and having to live by his wits rather than his humour. All in all, Tony Collins and Bill Shankley enjoyed a genuine friendship for many years and there is no doubt that such a friendship helped Tony in pursuing his long career in the game.

~~~~

Alan Dicks: The partnership with Dicks at Bristol was deemed by most to be a successful one. Alan was what Tony called a 'super salesman'. They held a professional level of respect for one another and managing a team in the first division with all that was going on in the boardroom and a decimated bank account was not easy. The directors and staff at Ashton Gate regarded Dicks and Collins as equals in many matters, but Dicks was the appointed manager and therefore looked to for the final opinion. They would of course have their disagreements; it would be impossible not to have the odd altercation in such a job where pressure was relentless and coming from all sides, and at the end of the day decisions are necessarily all about opinions. As a rule, whatever the final decision, they would both back one another in whatever needed to be said outside of the club gates. Being involved with football at any professional level is a very emotive job. Everyone needs to be right and everyone wants to win.

Tony had a close and separate bond with Alan and his family outside of the workplace. Alan's wife, Maura and their children always made him welcome and he particularly remembers a young Patrick 'Patch' who would shout 'It's bony Tony' through the letter box when he knocked their front door.

Gerry Gow (Gowie), was very much the find of Collins and looked to him for some form of direction if trouble loomed. However, Gowie and Dicks regularly 'locked horns' and on one particular day Dicks rang Collins looking for advice. Alan Dicks would always talk in terms of 'we' and 'ours' if there was in fact a problem. Tony remembers the conversation as follows:

'We've got a problem with Gowie coming to training. I can tell he's been drinking! What the hell are we going to do – confront him about it or just drop him?'

'Well, we need to keep him for this game. We can't afford for him to go absent. I think it's best to start him off on the bench!'

'There's going to be a bloody riot when his name isn't in the starting 11!'

'Leave it to me. I'll tell him!'

So Collins went out with the team for the relevant game and pulled Gow to one side.

'How's it going Gerry?' Collins asked.

'Alright thanks Tony,' Gowie replied knowing by the very fact that Tony was talking to him before the game that he had been rumbled. However, there was a level of respect between the two individuals that would allow the following instruction to go unchallenged.

'Gerry, you're on the bench to start off with. Let's just see how it goes.'

'OK Mr Collins,' came the cautious and possibly unexpected reply.

Dicks waited for the fireworks, looking over anxiously in their direction. But none came and the game started. After about 15 minutes, Collins said to Gow:

'Go and have a warm up; a few sprints and stretches down to the corner flag and back.'

So off went 'Gowie' expecting to get on to the pitch. When he came back, Tony told him to sit down. After another 10 or 15 minutes, Tony told him to get warmed up again. He did as asked and when he arrived back at the bench, Tony asked him to sit down. Gerry, by this time, was becoming wound up with Tony prepared to give him a verbal lashing if he let go.

The second half came round with a quietly boiling Gerry Gow taking his place once more on the bench. Tony said:

'Go and get warmed up will you?' to Gerry; a nervous Alan Dicks watching from only a few feet away. He came over to Tony and said: 'You are going to have to put him on soon!'

Gowie came back in an obvious mood and before he could say anything Tony told him to sit down and that the next time would probably be about right. Several minutes later at the nod from Collins, Alan Dicks put Gerry Gow on the pitch. The pent up tension and energy within the man, carefully massaged by the actions of Tony Collins became an immediate driving force as he began to carve up the midfield like a man possessed. The matter of Gow's drinking and late training appearances never needed to be mentioned again. The job had been done; the lessons learnt and all without any upset.

The signing of the Ritchie brothers, Stevie and Tommy, for Bristol was also a bit problematic from Dick's point of view. Everyone seemed to want Stevie, Tommy's younger brother who was only 15 and a Scottish schoolboy player. Their parents, Bob and Julia had their family house at Bo'ness on the south bank of the Firth of Forth in Scotland and Bob was a painter on the bridge, a dangerous job at any time of the year but a real killer in winter. One day when Tony and Bob were watching a game play involving Stevie, Bob mentioned that Tommy was a handy player too. So Tony told him to get the lad into his kit and get on the field. Tony was impressed and said so to Alan Dicks.

Alan didn't really want both players and needed some persuading. Bob and Julia also needed some convincing as they did not want their two only sons living some several hundred miles away from home. So,

Tony suggested to Alan Dicks that the whole family be given a club owned house and they could all move to Bristol. It was a master stroke. The Ritchie brothers were signed and their family moved down to Bristol. A level of trust had built up particularly between Tony and Tommy Ritchie after some weeks of close association. When there was a question to ask, Tommy would ask it of Tony. The house the Ritchie family had moved into was seen to have some damp problems and this was passed on to Tony to see what could be done about it.

Tony took the problem to Alan Dicks, who simply held his hands in the air as if to say 'what next?' Tony explained to Alan quite forcefully that the Ritchie family didn't leave a damp house in Scotland and so didn't expect to have to put up with one in Bristol. Whatever Alan Dicks saw wrong in the deal, most commentators and pundits were firmly of the view that Ashton Gate only took in both brothers to get their hands on the one – Stevie! However, the decision to take both proved to be the right one with the name of Tommy Ritchie now firmly engraved in the hearts of all Bristol City fans. The family still live in the Bristol area and Tony and his family have always called in on them on their way down to their favourite holiday spot in Cornwall.

Alan Dicks knew well the vagaries of professional football accepting that success would bring with it kind and encouraging words; support from some unexpected places and, most importantly, more bums on seats. He was an excellent 'front man', something Tony Collins was perhaps not. They spent much time together discussing players, budgets and tactics, despite the fact that Tony lived a few hundred miles away from Bristol and both made particular efforts to distance themselves from boardroom upsets as much as possible in order to deny individual directors the opportunity to perhaps divide and conquer. Alan is quoted as saying that he used to lighten the load with players by having some 'fun' things happen in training – and this was certainly true. Generally, Alan was a nice guy, dedicated to the game, who spent 13 years at Ashton Gate striving for success against all the odds – and got there. So just imagine what he could have achieved with some support from a dedicated, co-operative board and some money in the bank! There is currently a campaign (2015) led by the Bristol Post to recognise the work Alan Dicks did to make Bristol what it became in the day with comment about Tony Collins being the best scout in the game at the time.

Well, this was definitely true and as a team, Dicks and Collins; Manager and Assistant Manager, took Bristol City to the glory of top flight football in the 70's, an achievement that eluded the Directors and fans at Ashton Gate for another 30 years.

~~~~

Don Revie: Where to start with Don Revie. To Tony, Revie was, in his own words, '*the* top man' and they had a long, close working and personal relationship. Don offered the most enthusiastic encouragement to Tony with regard to his ability to write and produce such detailed and accurate reports on matches and players. He would tell people, with some pride, that he had waited five years to get hold of Tony and regularly made reference in public to Tony's near encyclopaedic knowledge of the game. Tony's opinion was that Don would never let a 'pal' down and no matter what the press said about Revie after leaving the England Manager's job; he was a man of his word and respected those around him who gave him their support. He was also a generous man and despite the Cloughism of the 'Damned United' and other manager's mutterings of 'Dirty Leeds', he took Leeds United where they had never been before – and was proud of it.

Action on the pitch was often hard when playing Leeds, but in those days, for many, English football was a hard game - played by hard men!

Tony recalls one day when the team were doing well and sitting top of the league, Don came into the office and said to all the backroom staff: 'Let's all go to York races – and I'll provide the kitty!'

Tony said that he couldn't go because he had a match to go to that evening. Don said: 'Tell Edith you'll be late home for tea. Come on, we are *all* going.'

They did – and had a great time.

There was very much a family spirit at Elland Road when Don was in charge, something that could not be re-created by Brian Clough, who always seemed to feel the spirited ghost of Don freely wandering the corridors and quietly invading the dressing rooms.

Tony and Don worked closely together in ensuring that detailed dossiers were maintained on every team Leeds would play both in England and overseas. Tony's match reports were faultless and they would both spend many hours discussing them and the tactics required to keep Leeds on top whether away or at Elland Road.

When Don told Tony he was considering taking the England manager's job, Tony remained quiet for some time. Don eventually pushed him to make some kind of comment.

'Do you really know what you're doing Don?' Tony asked.

'How do you mean Tony,' replied a curious Revie.

'Well, in my opinion, the England team are simply not good enough at the moment and if you take this job, you may be on a hiding to nothing – and it could go badly for you!'

'You may well be right Tony, but let me ask you this – how on earth can I really refuse?'

Don Revie accepted the job and then the nightmare started. The England campaign for the next three years would turn out to be disastrous and things at Leeds United would end up being not much better. The chairman of the Football league at that time was Alan Hardaker and it was an open secret he was no admirer of Revie. Sir Harold Thomson, chairman of the Football Association (FA) was also a difficult character to handle allegedly making mischief for Revie and attempting to possibly display influence in areas of the England Football Managers job that could be considered intrusive. The ridiculous affair surrounding his resignation as England Manager ended up with a public spat by the FA in suspending Revie from football for 10 years. The court case that followed overturned the politically motivated action and off he went to Dubai to manage the national UAE team.

Don and Tony had discussed the England situation on a few occasions as Tony still scouted for Revie whilst he was England manager. Tony was never very forward in 'diving in' to the 'goodies' on offer after an International game and this had been noticed by Don. After one match between England and Italy Don came up to Tony and said: 'You had better hang on to this – everyone else is grabbing bits and pieces!'

It was the Italian shirt of Francesco Graziani and the action by Revie was that of a man who cared, keeping his eye on all things happening around him. He was definitely no fool and certainly not mean as many who did not know him would label him. Don did not really want to take the job of managing the Emirates. However, a very substantial amount of money was on offer in an attempt to put the UAE into the International footballing arena with a squad of part timers who spoke very little English and were more interested in where the latest model Mercedes was coming from than getting fit for a football match.

However, Don Revie did in fact get on very well with the local

Arab royalty, especially Sheik Mana, who had his own football club called Al Nasr and after his short time with the national team, Don would go and manage Al Nasr on behalf of the Sheik. Don took Les Cocker with him to provide the fitness and training routines. Les seemingly enjoyed his time in Dubai for a couple of years and Tony was invited out to the desert state many times by Don telling him about a substantially improved lifestyle insisting that part of the dream of sun, sand and a lot of cash could be his. Reluctantly, although Tony loved Don, he loved the English game of football better and therefore never did go to Dubai — even to just visit.

~~~~

Brian Clough: The well known tenure of 44 days and the phrase 'Damned United' conjure up a picture of a football manager with a problem. Brian Clough didn't just have one problem — he had them in spades when he moved to Leeds United as manager after the departure of Don Revie in July 1974. Much has been said of Clough and his famous 44 days in charge at Leeds and much was made of his history of severe public criticism with regard to Revie's tactics in grooming what Clough regarded as a brutal team of players on the pitch.

Clough had taken Derby County from a sticky survival in the second division to the top of the first division, but like Ferguson, he was definitely a Marmite character – you either loved him or hated him! The Derby chairman was not too keen on his brash, authoritative ways and buying players for record fees without consulting the board of directors set a pattern of head to head confrontation. Eventually, Clough walked out on Derby, taking Peter Taylor and just about all the backroom staff with him. Such was the strange level of loyalty he generated amongst his staff but found difficult to emulate with many of his players. His next stop was Brighton & Hove Albion but his tenure was unexpectedly short, as was the team's ability to score goals and so when he arrived at Leeds, his life had been surrounded by turmoil for some time.

Tony and Clough got on well together as far as the game of football went, but Tony was not too keen on Clough as a person. He did not have Peter Taylor with him on his excursion to Leeds – and it showed. He liked a drink as well, which did nothing to calm an already hot headed personality. Tony thought he had too much 'swank' about him. Tony said; 'He would ask for an opinion on something and then just say 'right then' as he walked away leaving you not knowing what his thinking was.'

He seemed to be obsessed with the shadow of Don Revie and refused to sit in Don's old chair. He could also be verbally nasty to people, Tony included, when things did not go exactly his way. Tony remembers it was a difficult six weeks and the players were not happy.

However, whatever the public persona of Brian Clough, he certainly was a personality to be reckoned with. In his book he writes kindly of his experiences with Tony Collins and in a video recording of Clough, expounding on his time at Leeds, he recalls Tony as a gentle, softly spoken man being the only person who tried to turn him round and in effect attempted to stop him from making a complete fool of himself. He admitted that Tony had tried to slow things down a bit and that if he had listened, things might very well have been much different.

The book entitled 'The Damned Utd' by David Peace, was claimed by the publishers to be fact based fiction, but neither Tony Collins or Johnny Giles thought so, with Giles successfully suing Faber and Faber in an attempt to put the record straight. When the film of the book came out, it was acclaimed by many for the acting, but not by so many for its historical accuracy. As far as Tony Collins was concerned, Clough may have been a handful but he was not the rather dark character shown in the film. When he left; like everything else he did in his life, it was 'in style' as he picked up a cash figure that some say was very near to £100,000, an exceptionally large sum of money for the time and near to a million pounds at today's value.

~~~~

Alex Ferguson: Much has been said about Ferguson already. What did Tony Collins really think of him? Well, from Tony's point of view, he was not a man you could get into conversation with. He was simply not approachable and worked at staying that way. It appeared he wanted everyone's knowledge but didn't want to put his name to anything until it was a proven success. That was certainly true of player signings. Perhaps that's why he kept Archie Knox with him who was a totally different character.

Ferguson was also well used to sending mixed messages to the media, especially on subjects that would rotate around his staff. For example, in one article by David Meek of the *Manchester Evening News*, he encouraged the theory that it was his singular and therefore most shrewd decision to leave the backroom staff in place, including Tony Collins. The only new addition was to be Archie Knox who replaced Ron Atkinson's Mick Brown. However, only a matter of some months afterwards, Ferguson would be quoted as saying he was unimpressed with the Man United scouting network, a pointed dig at Collins. In his book 'Six Years at United' he lambasted Ron Atkinson for leaving behind what he intimated was possibly an unfit team that drank too much, backed up by a scouting operation that was not up to the job. Everything that Ferguson perceived to be a problem at United was everyone else's fault but his own. This was the view as far as Tony was concerned and there were others who thought so too. He was also a manipulator of the press and although perhaps even he would admit that communications were not his strong point, he often released information in such a way that put him in a certain light. A good example is the signing of teenager Lee Sharpe in the summer of 1988 and a later press report by John Bean in the *Daily Express* would cloak the whole episode in mystery inferring that Ferguson was some kind of wizard who dealt in dark and mysterious places rather than simply having a deal put in front of him that was a no-brainer. It described the manager of Torquay United, Cyril Knowles as 'scared out of his wits' and the passing of 'mysterious messages' and 'concealed identities'. By the end of the piece, one would have thought that Alex Ferguson was in fact the James Bond of football rather than being someone with a thick over-the-border accent, who spoke very little unless it was in disparaging terms about the poor performance of his staff. So what really did happen in the Lee Sharpe transfer? Well, these are Tony's own words, written and recorded after the event.

'I was at Manchester United for over six years as chief scout and in that time, the club seldom lacked a bob or two. Big money signings were always plentiful at Old Trafford. But United were not only interested in expensive million pound players and Alex Ferguson made it clear, as did Ron Atkinson before him, that they wanted to find some good youngsters too.

Len Noad, a well known sports writer in Manchester for many years had retired to Newton Abbott. He had been a great friend of mine and Jimmy Murphy for many years and still kept in touch with the game, keeping his eyes open for me. Len called me one day and said: 'Tony, I've been trying to find you a player for six years and I think I may have found one. His name is Lee Sharpe and he's playing outside left for Torquay. He's only sixteen years old, but he looks to have something.'

There and then, I decided to go and see him play on the following Friday night. I arranged to stay with Len and we set off for the match together. For twenty minutes the boy had not touched the ball and I saw Len look at his watch and knew what was going through his mind. He was thinking: 'I've brought him all this way and the lad is not going to do anything!' Having seen this situation many times before, I was not unduly bothered. Eventually he received a couple of balls that he controlled well and set off showing good pace and ability to take on an opponent. In the second half, although not in the game a lot, he did receive enough service for me to be able to recommend him, taking into consideration the boy's age of only 16. Although not outstanding, he had shown good control and skill, good vision and pace, unafraid physically and showing good stamina. I told Ferguson he ought to see him, and he agreed.

With Ferguson and Archie Knox, the three of us set off to meet Len Noad who I had asked to get four tickets for the game sitting two and two. I sat with Len. I also booked Ferguson and Knox in a hotel in Babbacombe in different names. We arranged to meet ten minutes before the end of the game at the car where we discussed Sharpe. There was a suggestion to wait until Tuesday to see him play against Newport and I advised strongly against it. So, eventually, after some discussion, we agreed to make an effort to sign the boy. Len went ahead after the crowd had gone and told Cyril Knowles that Alex Ferguson would like a word with him and that he was waiting in his car outside the ground.

Cyril Knowles was naturally surprised at the timing of it all and we agreed to meet him in another Babbacombe hotel to clinch the deal. To do so, Alex did in fact meet with Sharpe in the early hours of

Saturday morning. The overall deal was around £200,000 in a package and we all felt the price was right for a boy with potential and at the very least, we knew we would eventually get our money back.

It was decided to let Lee Sharpe stay at Torquay until the end of the season and a few days later, when Torquay played Newport, our South Wales scout rang me to say that Torquay had scored six goals against Newport and the radio reporter had said it was the 'Lee Sharpe show' that night. By then of course, we had nipped in to sign him but only in the nick of time. I dare say that by the end of the season, we might have had to pay double for him; it was just another case of moving at the right moment.'

The deal with Knowles to buy Sharpe was indeed discussed in the back of Ferguson's car but the arrangement was finalised in detail in a hotel with Cyril Knowles, the club secretary and Lee Sharpe in attendance. It was also near to one o'clock in the morning when the relevant hands were shaken and a price confirmed of £60,000 down. There was no 'cloak and dagger' scenario and Ferguson was far less than a James Bond character through it all. In fact, there was some definite hesitation and a desire to wait until Ferguson had a chance to see Sharpe in another game the following Tuesday. That hesitation was certainly not displayed by Tony Collins, in fact just the reverse and unless Tony had pushed for the signing that night, it may never have happened. So, it was Tony Collins who originally found Sharpe through his long established contact with Len Noad and it was also Collins who insisted Ferguson should not allow the talented boy to slip through their fingers. From all the evidence provided by Ferguson, it would be difficult to confirm that Collins was actually involved in the signing at all, but he in fact started it and was there, in the car with Ferguson and present through the negotiations with Knowles.

It is often forgotten that Ferguson was not the instant success that many thought he was and from taking over the reins in 1986 it took several seasons for the team to be re-organised enough to win the League Cup in 1992 and the Premier League in 1993. The years in-between were fraught with poor performances and a rumour mill generating constant warnings that the board were not happy. Martin Edwards, the chairman, was a tough cookie. He had collected £2.3 million for the sale of Mark Hughes to Barcelona in 1986 after a disastrous attempt to sell the club to Robert Maxwell in 1984 and he expected the appointment of Ferguson to immediately add energy to the club and increase those all important gates. But it didn't happen and neither did another attempt to sell the club once again to wealthy developer Michael Knighton. The first few years of Ferguson's tenure were therefore fraught with danger led by a chairman desperately trying to sell the club with one hand and push it to the top of the Premier League with the other.

The pressure was obviously there and Tony felt it as much as anyone else. However, as noted in previous chapters, Ferguson appeared not to have a management grip on the essential and most important aspect of the club, which was to trade players. In his book 'Six Years at United' he pointed another finger at Tony Collins regarding events surrounding his interest in John Barnes whilst the player was at Watford. He stated that Tony had only two reports on Barnes, which was a 'disappointment' and after sending Tony off to see Barnes play against Norwich he never received any 'strong indication' from the scouts that Barnes should be signed. He was probably well advised to add that as a 'relative newcomer' to the game of 'English football', he needed guidance!

Making excuses that the players he actually had were a bunch of drunken, aged has-beens did not allegedly wash with Edwards. He wanted results. In the end, the chairman solved his financial problems by floating United on the stock exchange, but this would prove to be only a temporary solution. In 1989, the chairman issued one or two statements assuring the press and the fans that Ferguson was not going to be sacked, but listening to the fans on the terraces, not only did they want Ferguson to go, they were shouting for Edwards to join him. The whole problem was put down to injuries of key players but at the heart of the issue lay the fact that Ferguson and Edwards did not have the money to buy players to beef up the squad so it would be relatively immune to such problems. Words of warning issued by Tony Collins to a stubborn and slippery manager fell mainly on deaf ears and it was no real surprise that Tony was eventually asked to go.

~~~~

Allan Clarke: Tony thought of Allan as a great player who never really did get his head round management. Although they had a good working relationship, Tony was not over keen on him as a person and he was always in a hurry to say 'no' before giving consideration to any particular proposal. The backroom boys called Clarke 'Goofy' and he was known to be something of a loner. Hailed as a hero by Leeds fans when he took up the role of manager, several games into the 1980-81 season, the bad start evened out to a better finish. The loss of Paul Madeley to injury was indeed a bitter blow and with Eddie Gray moved to left-back Clarke was expecting to bring the tilting ship upright again. There were conversations of course between Tony and Allan during this tense period, in fact there were many of them. As a result, Tony left, along with other backroom staff in 1981. The signs were all there and Allan was probably left in denial. Perhaps he had been influenced by someone such as Brian Clough in terms of how he dealt with players but seemed to miss the inspirational value that Clough could provide to a team when the chips were down.

However, the backroom had been cleaned out; the downward slide halted and as far as Clarke thought, the next season would hold great promise for Leeds United and its new manager. But the big issue would prove to be a defence unable to stop goals being scored against them and so good money was paid for the services of Kenny Burns to plug the gap. Gates were dropping, in some cases below 15,000 and the directors were looking for input from someone. It was obvious that Alan Clarke had no answers and so he left at the end of the '82 season to spend his next with Scunthorpe United.

~~~~

Ron Atkinson: To Tony, 'Big Ron' was one of the 'good blokes' and he enjoyed working with him. He had tremendous presence, a good knowledge of not only the game but many other subjects as well and he had a useful memory, something that always stood him in good stead. He would take notice of what you had to say and always come straight at you with a question. Ron and Tony had bumped into one another a lot over the years.

One evening Tony was out to see a West Bromwich Albion game during Ron's stewardship. The team he was proposing to send out included Bryan Robson and Remi Moses. He asked Collins what he thought.

'Very good Ron,' Collins told him.

'Mind you, the little fella (Moses) has had a few poor games lately – and I might leave him out.'

'Why would you do that,' said Tony 'he's enjoying himself and who else have you got in that position that has recently done better?'

On leaving the game, Ron told Tony he would be in touch and he was a man of his word as would shortly be demonstrated. They both got on well, had a similar sense of humour and most importantly, they both liked attractive football played with flair and skill.

The names of Robson and Moses were to flavour the conversation later when Ron Atkinson took over as manager of Manchester United in 1981. Ron once again asked Tony what he thought about each player. Tony told him he thought Ron should take them as a pair saying: 'They would be like a couple of 'body snatchers' together in midfield!'

So it was that Ron Atkinson signed them both for United and they were no doubt superb together. Tony's philosophy was that when a great player emerges like Bryan Robson, there also needs to be someone around him like Remi Moses. Midfield players often considered it difficult to find breathing space so they should in effect work in tandem. Moses and Robson, working together, cleared out the midfield in every game and were seemingly unbeatable until Moses received a bad injury.

Ron's father was also a bit of a character and made his presence known in the directors lounge on many a happy occasion. Manchester United, under the shepherding management of Ron Atkinson, was a great place to work. There was always a bit of a 'buzz' about the place and simply because of Ron's personality and sense of humour, the whole of Old Trafford was alive. He spent five fruitful years at United and felt that all he had spent there in monetary terms had been gained back. The team were definitely one of the very best supported during Ron's time at Old Trafford and he was proud of that statistic. In the 83-84 Cup Winners Cup quarter final, playing against Barcelona and the infamous Maradona, the attendance was estimated at around 60,000 but it sounded like twice that number inside the ground. Bryan

Robson remembers the pitch nearly 'shaking' with the roar and energy of the crowd.

However, Ron had his problems as do we all, and shortly after the Barcelona match, with a marriage on the rocks he received an approach from the Catalans. With some extended discussions about the length of any proposed contract becoming a stumbling point for Ron, the Spanish side began to feel that Atkinson was possibly trying to put himself into a strengthened negotiating position with the board at United and therefore the talks failed to reach any suitable conclusion. However, this whole series of events did not dull the energy of an inspired Atkinson, pushing the team to win the FA Cup the following season. Eventually however, with all that was happening in his private life, in 1986, when United failed to settle into an acceptable position in the league, Martin Edwards decided it was time for Ron to go. Perhaps the way he did it was of more hurt to Ron than the act itself and he said later that he had never thought of himself as a United manager for ten years, twenty years or for life and nor did he ever want to.

His record at "The Red's" was a good one with a success rate of 50% compared to Fergusons 59.6%. He was and still remains proud of what he did at Manchester United and his energy and humour will not be forgotten by those who worked with him during his time as manager. His marriage did sadly break up and a new one started with Maggie; one that has been proven by the test of time.

~~~~

Jimmy Murphy: Here was someone who was the great Sir Matt Busby's right hand man and Tony recalls that in effect Matt made him assistant manager. Murphy is best recognised as being a strong and thereby significant figure at Manchester United from an almost career spanning 1946 until the 1970s. He held roles such as assistant manager, chief reserve team manager, chief coach and a full-time scout. He also managed the Welsh National team from 1956 to 1964. Jimmy was the kind of person who shunned the limelight and preferred to work quietly behind the scenes. As a result of the Munich air disaster on 6 February 1958, Murphy was asked to take over the reins as Manchester United manager until the end of the 57-58 season and navigating the club through its greatest crisis.

Murphy had fortunately not been on the Munich aeroplane, as he had missed the trip due to a pervious engagement as manager of Wales who were playing Israel in Cardiff. When Tony Collins was appointed as Chief Scout at United, he and Jimmy became firm friends. They already knew each other quite well as Tony had always made Jimmy welcome if for any reason he wanted to pop into Old Trafford and have a chat. They held a certain level of respect for each other and Jimmy would regularly offer his services if Tony ever needed them. He was also a person who would often become involved in scouting and he and Tony would spend many hours chatting about players and their potential. Tony felt on several occasions that Sir Matt may not have quite looked after Jimmy as he might. However, he was a loyal servant to the team and to his manager Matt Busby; never wishing to hear a disparaging word against either.

Tony recalls Jimmy as great, super, straight as a die, and no one would run Matt down in front of him. Jimmy said to Matt one day about a particular player 'He's a comedian' and Matt's astute reply was 'Don't knock the comedians Jim.' One half of the Charlton bothers, Bobby, whose career with United spanned from 1956 to 1973, also held the managing team of Sir Matt and Jimmy with a certain amount of respect telling Tony that 'While ever Matt is at United – I'm safe.' His brother, 'Big Jack' who played for Leeds United from 1952 to 1973, also held the pair in high esteem and in Tony's opinion, perhaps such a successful and formidable pairing will never be seen in English football again. Jimmy Murphy sadly passed away in November 1989.

~~~~

Manny Cussons: This was a man considered to be quite a character. He had made a fortune in the retail business and had an amazing head for figures and business in general. He was chairman of a major Leeds based furniture trading outlet and he could walk around his store and calculate the value of the stock on display within a few pounds. He famously became chairman at Leeds United from 1972 to 1983 and one day invited Tony Collins to his Leeds store. They both stood on a balcony overlooking the shop floor and Manny turned to Tony and said 'What do you think?' Tony replied respectfully, 'Very nice Mr Cussons, but I can't afford much of this on my wages'. Message received loud and clear!

At another time when Leeds were on tour, the team and staff were staying at a top hotel somewhere on the continent. Manny in his normal manner was totting up the cost of the stay, when one of his fellow directors said, 'Why don't you buy the place Manny?' and without a second's thought he turned round and said 'What ... and have all my relatives want to come and stay for free?' Manny was a decision maker and a tough character as witnessed by all at Elland Road in the Clough situation. Tony liked his style and his determination.

CHAPTER FIFTEEN

Player and Match Reports Written By the 'Master Spy'

Tony Collins had a long and distinguished career as a scout for talented players working for all the top teams of the day including the England side for several years. He would travel endlessly to matches up and down the country and watch established professional players, emerging players and talented schoolboys with the aim of seeking out the next signing before the competition.

Tony Collins was not the only scout in the business of course. There were many, and each league team would have its own chief scout and possibly a small team of one or two others to back him up. Each scout would have their own connections on the coaching staff of established teams, sports reporters and school Physical Education specialists. Tony spent many years building up a set of nationwide connections across a broad spectrum of 'spotters', keeping him usually one step ahead. This involved building up a team of fifteen to twenty scouts in all regions of the country. He was probably the most written about scout in the profession for nearly twenty years. What Tony Collins said about the game of football mattered – and when he had something to say, most people in the business listened. He was in the sporting headlines and quoted by reporters on a near weekly basis and no one in such a position within the game has ever received such attention either before or since.

So maybe the publishing of some fascinating, but up to now secret reports, on players he has watched and studied over the years will provide a level of insight as to Tony's ability to appraise a player, not only for his talent with the ball, but regarded with just as much importance would be the individual's depth of character.

~~~~

Gordon McQueen: The first report relates to Gordon McQueen playing as a 20 year old for Tommy Bryceland's St Mirren who was first reviewed by Collins in a match where they played Colchester in a pre-season friendly. Tony had already seen him play at a private practice match with Celtic on Wednesday July 26th with a final score of 4-2 to Celtic. Naturally, a full and detailed report had been written and Gordon played first class football for many years. He was bought by Leeds United for around £30,000 finally making his most expensive move from Leeds to Manchester United in 1978 for a figure declared to be near to half a million pounds sterling. He also played for the national team of Scotland. The unedited report below is reproduced in Tony's own words.

Result: Colchester 2 – St Mirren 0. Date: Monday August 7th, 1972. Conditions: Warm, sunny evening. Pitch: Fairly small but very good turf.

'St Mirren lost this game through bad finishing up front and poor defensive play at the back, even though they were the more controlled side when in possession for long periods. Colchester were young and they made up in endeavour what they lacked in skill. For a friendly match, the game had quite a bit of bite.'

'Players Under Review for St Mirren were Centre Half McQueen at 6'1" tall, well built and naturally left sided. The player will pass and clear ball off his right side and he showed good turn of speed coming forward and in recovery. His kicking was good and powerful, although not always accurate. Passing was firm and definite and he won nearly everything in the air that was played up from defence. He had a bad night with crosses. Some he headed away with power, but generally the balance was against him. Sometimes he allowed opponents to get in behind him, but in the main it's because he does not position himself correctly in the first place. Often he is caught shallow. Put himself on the goal line for corners against, because an average height centre forward stood there. He could have detailed somebody else to do that job. On a few occasions, he was pulled away from the man he was marking by a bad shout of "up big fella" by the goal keeper to go and head a ball six yards away for a player who already had his opponent marked. On the odd occasion, he arrived late. If the ball had gone to the man he had left, it would have caused no end of trouble. The goal keeper was also calling him to go for balls that he should have got himself. Because he is tall, the defence and goal keeper is expecting him to do everybody's work in the air. He gets a lot of bad advice. At times he called defence up from the middle of the field when he was not the last man. Made some good interceptions but marred a few by bad lay-offs. Ran back off the ball once or twice without looking back at the ball. Does not drop off enough when attacking to receive or when defending to collect. Plays too shallow. Made some good tackles from the side, but missed a few face on. Those he won face on were often with a struggle. Caught opponent in the head trying to recover when a long ball bounced past them. Picked his ball up well when clearing off the floor. Showed good control. Needs lessons in containing. Taken way out past near post for some throws, when someone else could have done that job. Courageous boy, taking a diving header across opponents boot to get ball away. He is hard enough. Lacks experience. Only been playing eighteen months to two years. Playing in goal at one time. Only played six matches as a junior. For all his shortcomings, I still feel he has a lot of natural ability and would be a calculated risk worth taking at the price I mentioned initially – twenty to twenty five thousand. Sold himself for 2nd goal. Beaten by a 1-2 ball. Met his father, who told me that the boy has been sick before matches recently in view of his impending transfer.'

As can be seen by the last comment, Tony had already discussed the player with his Leeds backroom staff and the ending comment in his July report stated that:

'For all his faults, he is playing in a defence that has no system and cannot play. He will learn nothing playing with these players. Still has good ingredients for the position.'

Tony's thoughts about McQueen were by now obvious, but what about the element of 'character'? The following week Tony took a look at McQueen again, but this time in a match against Rangers and in what Tony described as 'heavy, driving rain'. He noted the following:

'This game was won and lost in the first twenty minutes by Rangers going into an early two goal lead. The first goal came in ten minutes through C.H. Ure. The Rangers goal keeper had the ball in his hands and Ure called everybody up. The ball was kicked a long way down the field and Ure completely misjudged the bounce to allow Johnston, the Rangers inside forward to run on and score. The second goal was scored a few minutes later and from then on it was one way traffic from the Rangers to the St. Mirren defence.'

The next paragraph of Tony's report on that match, specifically identifying the contribution by McQueen, was as follows.

'He gave Johnston (who is very quick) three yards start in fifteen and won the ball with a great tackle. His big problem is off the ball. He needs coaching in positioning. Sometimes he drops off deep to help others, other times he doesn't. Often does not drop off deep enough when own full back has the ball and is being pressured. Still feel the natural ingredients that he has are better than anything else I have seen so far. He tired in the last ten minutes, which is understandable when generally he was the only defender between the Rangers attacks and a lot more goals.'

So these are the thoughts of England's Master Spy when looking at a player who went on to achieve great things for Leeds United when Don Revie was looking for a replacement as good as Charlton; a tall order in anyone's book!

Steve Bruce: There were of course, many players viewed and analysed by Tony Collins who were not immediately recommended for inclusion in his teams at the time but were signed a couple of years later. A typical example is Steve Bruce, who at the time of writing (2015) is the manager of a first class side, Hull City. One of the earliest

Collins reports on Bruce was in October 1982 when he was playing for Gillingham. This was a Third Division side sitting at around 20 in the table and playing against Oldham Athletic in the second round of the Milk Cup. The result was Oldham 1 – Gillingham 0 and a six feet tall, 22 year old, 11 stone 6 lb Bruce was playing at left back. The player report started with a list of assessments.

His right foot was very good and assessed as his natural side with a fair left foot and not afraid to play off it. His tackling was considered strong and attitude to physical contact, very good. He enjoyed it! The climb to head was very good and only lost one ball in the air. The direction of heading was fairly good and speed average when coming forward. He never really turned in this game and a good change of pace was not in evidence. His ball control was average and reading of the game very good. His movement of the ball was good and passing fairly good. Irrespective of the above, he can play well. Part of the actual report is reproduced below.

'This match suited Bruce because Oldham played into them all night mainly hitting long balls into the heart of the Gillingham defence where Bruce won almost everything in the air and on the floor. He covered Shaw very well and used the ball when he could. On one of the few occasions Oldham missed him out with the ball they managed to score a goal. Nobody came off him and nobody turned him, making it difficult to assess whether he could cope with this situation and whether he has the pace.'

The next match Tony Collins reported on was Gillingham against Bradford City in January 1983. The result was a draw with one goal each and this is what Tony thought of Bruce's performance.

'This game was played in rain throughout. The pitch got cut up and very heavy. Bruce enjoyed the physical challenge. He is strong and won nearly all 50-50 tackles. There is a question on his judgement in the tackle. On the few occasions that Bradford's front men came off him, he allowed them to go and was caught ball watching on a few occasions from the cross. He defended well, but his distribution lacked accuracy under pressure, often making work for himself. His strength is his main asset. Although winning most balls in the air, he did not get a lot of distance. In the main he was just content to clear his lines. He needed time to control the ball.

Conclusions: He looked good when opponents played up close to him. Good when facing the play but inclined to panic under pressure. On this display he did not appear to have enough composure for the first division and did not have much around him in defence. This is the second viewing. His first game at Oldham was good, but Oldham played into him. Note: Will be seen again. No other outstanding players on either side.'

The next viewing of Bruce as a 23 year old was at an FA Cup match between Gillingham and Everton. The result was a goalless draw and considered to be well deserved by Gillingham playing against a First Division side and one that would go on to win the FA Cup that year.

'Gillingham well deserved their draw with their 'over my dead body' attitude. The Gillingham backs Bruce and Shaw took Everton's Gray and Sharpe out of the game. They battled for everything. Bruce competed well. Very strong and won most balls in the air although he turned his back at times, lacks patience. Powerful in air at set pieces, not quite tall enough to really dominate, winning ball by sheer desire.'

The final match where Bruce had been viewed by Collins was an afternoon Liverpool v Norwich clash at Liverpool on January 19th, 1985. Bruce had moved on from Gillingham and now played for Norwich at right or centre back. He was 24 years old and a fit six feet tall and still weighing 11 stone and six pounds. The result was a win for Liverpool and a score-line of 4–0. It was a cold and windy afternoon but the pitch was in good condition and Tony Collins reported as follows:

'Norwich played well in the first quarter of an hour and had Liverpool at full stretch, especially down the right side with Barham moving inside Kennedy and Deehan making late runs down the right flank. But Norwich had nobody to finish. Barham threatened a lot but never went by on his own. Deehan took a knock after twenty minutes and was hardly in the game after that. Liverpool scored five minutes before half time and the game was always in the balance until the last quarter of an hour even though Norwich had virtually no shots on target.

Norwich centre-back, Bruce was strong right sided and blasted everything away. He was wild at times, diving into tackles and is a brave player. He defended stubbornly and was a danger at all Norwich corners and free kicks. He was always flat out and allowed striker to come off him. He gave Rush free header for the 1st goal. Note: He gave 100% effort and is very strong but not the player we need. For Liverpool, Dalgliesh and Hanson were outstanding.'

The report on Steve Bruce, someone who, as previously stated would eventually go on to manage Hull City, was carefully filed back at

Manchester United HQ and perhaps when Ferguson was not in the mood to talk with his chief scout, maybe he investigated all the filed reports to create a wish list of his own. So, originally spotted by Collins, Bruce was contracted by Manchester United in December 1987. Certainly the proposed signing of this fine player was not discussed by Ferguson with Tony – or his staff, as far as he can remember.

~~~~

Trevor Francis: Not only young, up and coming players were assessed by Tony Collins and during his time with Manchester United he took a long look at Trevor Francis who was playing for Manchester City as a striker. He had transferred from Nottingham Forest managed by Brian Clough. The transfer fee was a record at the time and the first to break the one million pound ceiling. Clough, ever the showman, announced the deal dressed in his squash kit and appeared eager to get to his game. In 1981, Francis went to Manchester City for a reputed £1.2 million and on the 8th of May, 1982, Collins reviewed the performance of Francis, a million pound player, in a match against Coventry. The result was a poor performance by Manchester City with the score-line ending up 3–1 in favour of Coventry. The report details as written by Collins are reproduced below.

Francis was known to be aged 26, around 5'10 ½ tall and weighing in at 11 stone 7 lbs. His right foot was excellent and considered by Tony to be his natural side. His left foot was noted as fairly good and that he could cross accurately off this side. His tackling ability was deemed fair but he doesn't win many balls other than by his pace.

His attitude to physical contact was not the bravest and Tony Collins considered him not to be a particularly hard player. He seems to take a lot of knocks reasonably well. His climb to head was fairly good and direction of heading also fairly good when unchallenged. His speed was excellent along with his change of pace. He generally maintained very good acceleration, ball control and speed. His reading of the game appeared to be very good from a forward point of view. Movement off the ball was considered excellent as he sees openings well. His passing was very good generally and irrespective of the above, he can play well.

'General Report: Francis began the game playing in the centre and deeper than the other two strikers, he showed all the qualities that a top striker needs; vision, good control and pace plus excellent acceleration leaving defenders flat footed. He pushed more forward eventually, being very quick on the turn and coming off centre backs to peel off for ball up alongside. He takes opponents on and worries them all the time with his pace and quick change of direction. He made one break and shot against goal keepers legs, then scored from a cross to the far post where he pulled the ball down very quickly, moved inside a defender to place a low shot past the goal keeper. There is no question of his ability.'

During his short tenure with Manchester City, Francis made 26 appearances and scored 12 goals and playing for England he is credited with 52 appearances and 12 goals.

~~~~

Arnold Muhren: Another interesting player spotted by Collins was the Dutch midfielder Arnold Muhren. He went to see him play for Ipswich where he had been for some three years or so. The date was March 13th, 1982 and the game between Ipswich and Arsenal, which Ipswich lost

1–0. Tony noted the player to be 5'11" tall, weighing in at about 11 stone and approx 28 years old. He used his right foot only when pushed but his left foot provided an excellent touch on what was his natural side. Tony reckoned his tackling was almost non-existent and only made attempts to steal the ball. He didn't really like physical contact and although his climb to the head was fair, he seldom won a ball under challenge. His speed was average and change of pace good. Ball control was excellent off his left side and reading of the game fairly good from an attacking viewpoint.

'General Report: The very windy conditions made good football difficult. Muhren has good control; good vision and uses the ball well. He pulls wide on the left when team gets possession, opening up situations for others. He checks back inside when team loses possession, but really only fills space because his attempts at tackling are virtually non-existent. He was seldom in this game because the conditions being what they were, a lot of tackling was required. He really wins nothing in the tackle or in the air. He is essentially a forward player. He very seldom goes for a tackle at all, he just kicks through it. He makes token challenges. He makes good runs off the ball and his passing is well weighted and can pick his team mates out when crossing balls. Anybody taking him must use him for his forward play.'

It was unusual at that time to consider foreign players in the English League and after some discussion back at Old Trafford, Muhren was signed for Manchester United. He also played 23 games for the Netherlands scoring 3 goals, leaving Manchester for Ajax in 1985 where he would last out his playing days to the age of 38.

~~~~

Steve Hodge – Chris Waddle: With Manchester United being one of the biggest traders of players at the top end of the game, Collins, as part of his scouting duties, was kept busy reviewing player performances on the pitch, under pressure and in full on match conditions. Sometimes two players could be assessed at one time and so it was with Steve Hodge and Chris Waddle at a match between Newcastle and Nottingham Forest.

The date was October 20th, 1984 and the play was at Newcastle. Hodge was with Notts Forest at the time and Waddle with Newcastle. They had both been in place for a few years and both would go on to play for the England team. Hodge, born in Nottingham, played off his left foot as a midfielder and Waddle, who was also a local lad born in Tyne and Wear, played as a striker and would turn out to be the best player of the day from Tony's point of view.

It was a daytime match and the conditions were windy, cold and regular showers. The pitch was noted to be in good condition. Tony wrote as follows:

'This game was ruined by a very strong wind blowing straight down the pitch. Forest had the wind behind them in the first half yet Newcastle were well on top in the early phases. Forest took the lead just on half time through Hodge after centre back Hart hit a bad clearance for goal following a corner which Hodge scrambled over the line in a melee one yard out. Newcastle deservedly equalised ten minutes from time after good work on left by Waddle and Heard. Heard crossed ball to Wharton who struck the upright and followed in very quick to score. Notts Forest midfield player Hodge was seldom in the game but scored the goal. He made a very good run through the channels, got clear once but finished poor on his right side. Good left foot with controlled pace. He cannot win ball and has a very light frame. He followed ball when the team was in possession and at times closed the game up. Does not know how to make a space or release others but made one very good run on the ball past two defenders.

Note: Notts Forest — Hodge. I would not be over critical in these conditions but rarely in game. See again.

Newcastle striker — Waddle. Best forward on the pitch with good control, change of pace and a good run on an off the ball. The games best player with smart change of pace, good run on and off ball and generally very clever.'

Steve Hodge of course, went on to play for England as did Waddle who also played for some memorable teams such as Tottenham Hotspur and Sheffield Wednesday ending his professional career at Torquay United and continuing to play non-league football up until 2013/14 season.

~~~~

Gary Lineker: The first recorded and filed viewing and assessment of Gary Lineker was as a 23 year old, 11 Stone 10 lb striker for Leicester City. The game was a second division league match against Wolverhampton Wanders with a score line of 5–0 to Leicester.

'Conditions were ideal for football. Flat pitch, took a stud, no wind, mild afternoon. Wolves were completely outplayed by a more positive and sharper Leicester team. Lineker, playing off big centre forward Smith had an excellent game. Always prepared to run off Smith and come off centre backs for balls up alongside keeping the

Wolves back four turning. He had far too much pace for them. He played either side of Smith and brought a good save from a left foot shot by the bottom of the post in the first five minutes. He pulled away well when team mates came through middle on the ball. Scored from a few yards from pull back by Lynex and was unlucky not to score more goals. He won quite a few balls in the air because he held the ball up well in the box. He showed good awareness. On one occasion he came off to control the ball on his chest, turned inside then went outside and left Dodd by ten yards finishing with a good cross. Leicester football is more controlled now than the tearaway style of before and in this environment, they will produce better players. Note: Must be seen again on this showing.'

The next report on Lineker was a match where Leicester played against Southampton on 30th November 1983. It was an evening fixture and the pitch was noted to be in good condition. The two first division teams would have a battle on their hands with both eager to climb to the top of the league that season. The score was 2-1 in favour of Leicester and Lineker would score one well deserved goal.

'This was no game for faint hearted forwards. It was a battle from the start to finish with fouls by both sides. The match began at 7.45pm and half time came at 8.40pm because the trainers were on so often. Lineker showed very good pace. Everything about his opening spell was running off others. He never took opponents on. He came off centre backs and peeled off on odd occasions. Average control and very right sided. He got to the left goal line once with nobody near him but had to delay a cross, bringing the ball back to his right foot. He was injured after 15 minutes and looked as though he might come off. However, he carried on and scored a side foot goal from a low cross coming from the left about 4 yards out. He was taken off a few minutes later and would be doubtful for a game at Forest on Sunday.

Note: Injured early on and taken off 15 minutes in second half after scoring.

Southampton: Goalkeeper Shilton and forward Williams were their best players.'

The following report on Lineker was some months later on April 14th, 1984 when Leicester played Aston Villa with a final score of 2–0 in favour of Lineker's side.

'Lineker showed in this game all that has been seen before and no more. He runs well off striker Smith. If Smith is doing well then half his game is gone. His first touch is not generally good. He is a straight runner, lacks guile and has problems when trying to beat an opponent. His assets are pace and generally good finishing.'

You may note that Tony Collins didn't seem quite as happy with Lineker during this performance compared with earlier ones. However, the next viewing was a much more different game with Leicester playing Liverpool on the 18th of April, 1984. The finishing score was a draw at 3–3 in an evening match where the conditions were noted as fine and dry.

'This was an exciting game. Liverpool led early on then Leicester equalised taking the lead with Liverpool equalising again. Liverpool looked as if they would score whenever they got possession. Lineker showed very good pace but his initial control was loose. Passing under pressure was not good enough and did not win anything in the air. He cannot beat an opponent and lacks craft. His very good pace is his asset and does not often look for the ball in build up. His main play is running off striker Smith and even then his judgement and timing is often out.

Note: If he doesn't score you won't remember what he's done.'

The final viewing filed in the Manchester United player review records was in a match where Leicester played Nottingham Forest on May 5th, 1984. It was an afternoon conflict on a firm, flat pitch and the sun was shining.

'This was a hard fought game which Leicester deserved to win being the more enterprising side on the day. Forest continually broke down through poor final balls. They also missed Walsh on their left flank. Lineker was mainly blotted out of this game by Forest centre back Fairclough who was always quicker to the ball than Lineker. He hardly won a ball in the air from his defence; did not meet the ball well and his passing under pressure was poor. His control was poor yet he had a hand in the first goal and scored the second. For the first goal he laid a ball back to Ramsey who played the ball on for Lynex to score. The second goal was the only time he won a ball in the air touching it on to Smith who headed the ball on for return. Lineker burst through the defenders to push the ball past the goalkeeper. A typical Lineker goal, yet he had a bad game.

Note: He can stretch defence and will score goals but doesn't play generally with others.'

So, despite much consideration by Collins, who would have liked him to show a bit better form than he was seeing on that particular day; his opinion of Gary Lineker was not high enough to prompt him to recommend his possible purchase and move to Manchester United at that time. However, Gary went on to much greater things being sold to

Everton for a reputed £800,000 in 1985 and moving on to Barcelona in 1986. He also made over 80 appearances for England and eventually became a TV personality of major proportions gaining an MBE from the Queen in 1992.

~~~~

David Seaman: A left handed goal keeper who, on the pitch, favoured his right hand and foot was an unusual combination at the time. However, David Seaman played with those special talents for Peterborough United in 1983. He was only 21 years old but stood six feet three inches tall and weighed in at a comfortable 13 stone. The match reported on was a fourth division meeting with Bury at their Gigg Lane ground. Collins noted it was a cold, dry night with no wind and the pitch in good condition. The result was a 2–2 draw which was probably the right result.

'This was a very scrappy poor standard game. Peterborough slammed everything in the air to their tall strikers Hankin and Waddle. Bury did the same for their small strikers who won nothing in the air. Both teams played everything too early. It was just like watching a tennis match. David Seaman did not have a lot to do mainly having to collect long through balls from the Bury defence. His kicking was good, over ten yards beyond the halfway line off the floor and very long from his hands. Tall and right sided, he seldom threw the ball out; everything was played off the Peterborough front two. He was at fault with both Bury goals. The first was from a ball played down the side of his eighteen yard box almost to the goal line. He was first to the ball but appeared to let the ball run for a goal kick. Bury striker Madden got his foot to the ball to play it across the goal for Entwistle to score. The second came from a through ball to Jakub running away from the goal when he charged out and made a reckless tackle to give away a penalty. Note: Poor display being at fault with two goals. No outstanding players.'

Although Tony Collins was obviously not impressed at that particular time with David Seaman, (as often happens with young goalkeepers), he would improve and become a fine 'goalie' moving on to play for Manchester United in 2003. He also went on to appear for England in 1987 and pick up an MBE in 1997 for his services to sport.

~~~~

Garth Crooks: A sometimes controversial black player, Garth Crooks was playing for Tottenham Hotspur on the 3rd of September, 1983 when the team took on West Ham in a first division match. This fit striker weighed in at 11 stone and 6 lbs and standing five feet eight inches tall, was eager to get on with it.

The assessment was that his right foot was fairly good; not used a lot but accurate. His left foot was very good and this was his natural side. His tackling was fair but didn't challenge well. The attitude to physical contact was not strong and he didn't win many challenges. The climb to head was fairly good for his height. His direction of heading was good when best man, but happy enough to win the ball under challenge. His speed made him quick off the mark but faded on long runs. The change of pace was fairly good and ball control, good. His reading of the game was fairly good and movement off ball generally good to receive balls from defence, but not so good when playing off forwards. His passing was generally good and irrespective of the above, he can play!

'Conditions: dry and windy afternoon. Pitch in very good condition. Garth Crooks had a reasonable game (mainly outside the box) on very limited service. He had two good chances to hit the target. One free header put just outside the post and the other off a 1-2 inside the box, but delayed waiting for the ball to come on the left foot. He had three shots blocked inside the box. He came off back four well and played balls accurately off both sides. All front men suffered when coming off to receive through defenders carrying the ball too long. Made good runs as second man but seldom showed any thrust inside the box. He seldom won challenges for the ball and although he played neat and tidy balls off he never went by alone, generally allowing defenders to slow him down when running with the ball. He was fairly quick off the mark but not a lot of pace on thirty yard runs. Took up good positions initially but was seldom given the ball. He did not resist challenges too well, often finishing on the floor and he had more shots at goal than the other forwards. Spurs defenders did such a lot of long range shooting I suspect there was not enough bite in the box. Although not an outstanding game for him he should be seen again away from home. Note: Overall game reasonable on scant service. See away from home.'

Garth would go on to play for Manchester United on a loan agreement for a short period between November 1983 and January 1984. He would finish his footballing days with a knee injury in 1990 and go on to have a successful career in TV and Media.

~~~~

Peter Barnes: Was 25 years old when Collins saw him playing for Leeds United on the 27th of August, 1983 against Newcastle United. It was a second division match which Leeds lost 1–0 at Elland Road.

Barnes played outside left, stood at 5 feet 10 inches tall and weighed in at around 11 stone 2 lbs.

The assessment was that his right foot was fairly good and seldom used. His left foot was very good and this was his natural side. His tackling was almost non-existent. The attitude to physical contact appeared to be that he didn't relish it. The climb to head was poor unless unchallenged. His speed made him quick off the mark but faded on long runs. The change of pace was very good and ball control, very good but initial control loose at times. His reading of the game was fairly good and movement off ball indifferent, a mix of good and poor. His short passing was generally good but long passing lacked touch and accuracy, although irrespective of the above, he can play!

'Conditions: A warm, dry, sunny afternoon with a pitch in very good condition. Peter Barnes had a poor game considering the tremendous natural ability he possesses. With not being the challenging type, he has a lot to do when he is in possession. He played on both flanks and whilst he often turned his full back opponents he never went by at all in the first half and only went by once in the second. He never attacked the far post from crosses from opposite flank and won nothing in the air. He ran into trouble cutting inside, often running into second or third defender. He was sometimes left behind other forwards and watching them play. He took a long time to make his mind up on the ball. Often his brain does not tie up with his natural ability. Note: On this display he has a lot to do to get back to the first   division. For Newcastle, Keegan and McDonald played well.'

Barnes went on to play for Manchester United but became a victim of Ferguson's arrival. He also played for Manchester City being one of very few who had managed to play for both Manchester teams; his father Ken Barnes was City's chief scout. He toured many countries playing football eventually retiring to Malaysia and becoming a soccer commentator.

~~~~

Luther Blissett: This black footballer appeared to have a charmed life, being a Watford player who ended up in the front line squad for A.C. Milan. This was a club that had paid £1m for him in 1983 and then sold him back to Watford for about half that figure in 1984. He was a striker with a reputation and played for England between 1982 and 1984. The match Tony went to watch was a clash between England and Scotland at Hampden Park on May 26th, 1984. The fit looking 26 year old stood around five feet 10 inches tall and weighed in at an accommodating 11 stone 13 lbs. The pitch conditions were noted as good and it was a generally fine afternoon, with some later showers. The score would end up a draw at one goal each with both sides evenly matched.

'This was quite a good game for the end of season and it was good to see two teams going for a result. England outside left Barnes caused right back Gough a lot of problems when going at him, only thing was he didn't do it enough and final balls were not good. Playing two strikers, England caused Scotland problems not allowing Miller to sweep. Strachan was best midfield player in the first half making penetrating runs both on and off ball. It was a big surprise when subbed because Wark and Bett had hardly touched the ball. Scotland should have made more with having three in midfield. Scotland opened scoring from a clearance that eventually came to Strachan in a forward position. Blissett showed good pace and made space well by checking out or by peeling off and stretching defence. The first touch was not always good, but brave enough and he did not win much in the air, finishing on the floor at times in tight situations. Not afraid to take opponents on when he can get a run at them and not always successful. He worked very hard and will play others through, never giving up, thereby always in with a chance. He took McLeish on twice and left him for dead with shots blocked after. I would take him against Lineker. He's bigger, possibly braver and more importantly can play better with others. You can see him more in the game than Lineker. He is not a great player but at today's prices would give value for money considering the current dearth of top class players. Woodcock's goal was brilliant. He checked off Miller and Miller being afraid of the pace, let him go. Woodcock controlled the ball and ran at him turning him inside out two or three times before moving across his face to hit a left foot shot inside the near post with the goalkeeper moving away. Note: Blissett striker for A.C. Milan and value for money at £300,000.'

So it looks like the uncertainty within A.C. Milan about whether or not they had spent wisely on Blissett had perhaps prompted Tony Collins to report on the player with a view to possibly buying him. Certainly the price was right for Manchester United and it's interesting to note that Tony thought the skilful Jamaican a better buy than Lineker. The next viewing of Blissett would be when England played Russia at Wembley on June 6th, 1984. The pitch was in good condition and the day was noted as fine. The score line ended up at 0–2 favouring Russia.

'Although the wrong result it was an interesting game. England played 4-2-4 and Russia 1-3-4-2 with often the front two split up. England began quite bright with outside left Barnes looking dangerous and threatening but playing for himself, generally breaking down on the second or third opponent and eventually getting subbed. Chamberlain looked more dangerous today which goes to show the inconsistency at an International level of our players. The two centre backs were awful, not being able to control or read unusual situations. Blissett generally had a good game; still didn't win much in the air but showed good ability to make space by checking or peeling off. Fell over at times in tight situations but showed passing ability once he had the ball under control and played some well weighted through balls. Had a few good shots on target but didn't hit them at full force appearing to lack a bit of confidence in this area probably due to his lack of goals in Italy. The Russians began to dominate once they had sized up the midfield situation of four against two. Shilton gave a superb display saving us from an even heavier defeat. Duxbury was at fault with the first goal, treading on a long ball from the Russian goalkeeper to allow sub Gotsdnov to run on and score. Duxbury should have taken the ball on his left foot but put his right foot across. The second goal was from a long kick by the Russian goalkeeper and Fenwick, instead of closing for an aerial battle, dropped off allowing a Russian striker to play Blokhin who accelerated beyond Duxbury (who should have covered) to shoot. Shilton diverted the shot but could not recover to stop Protasov, (another sub) to score. Blissetts's first touch was often loose but showed good pace and strength and often not played early enough by Wilkins in particular when checking out. Overall, Blissett had a good match. On this display would take him against Regis on ability but also on difference of fee. Note: A.C. Milan striker Blissett in advance of Regis on this display plus the difference in fee required.'

On this reading, it looks as if Blissett was in the frame for a move to Manchester United. Ron Atkinson was well settled at United by the summer of 1984 and was probably looking for a striker with a bit of flair and to snatch someone who had sold for a million at a knock down price would have appealed not only to the manager but the directors as well.

Blissett would in fact move back to Watford after which his footballing career would start to slip downwards. Retirement from the game would push him toward becoming a sporting pundit for Channel 4 and Sky Sports. His interests would eventually turn in the direction of motor racing, a sport he is still heavily involved in today (2015).

~~~~

Charlie Nicholas: This was a Glaswegian born Celtic player in his third year with the team and first year playing for the full Scotland side. The following match would in fact be the first time he had been capped for the senior team and he would no doubt be out to impress. The date was 30th March, 1983 and the game was a European Championship match against Switzerland. The young impressive 21 year old striker weighed in at 11 stone and stood at five feet nine inches. This is Tony Collins report on an encounter that would result in a disappointing 2–2 draw.

His right foot was considered to be excellent and he dribbled off this side. His left foot was deemed to be fairly good on short passes and shots. Tackling was fair but he seldom wins a ball. He resists physical contact and doesn't challenge strongly. His climb to head was not good under challenge and direction of heading good when unopposed. His speed was good and change of pace very good. Ball Control was generally very good and reading of game also very good around the box. Movement of Ball was variable with good passing: Irrespective of above, he can play well.

'The match was played in cold wind and rain. For an hour Scotland did not look like a team and the service to the front men was poor and delayed. At the end of this period Scotland were losing 2–0. Then Wark scored for Scotland and Nicholas equalised with a well taken goal initially controlling the ball with his right foot and volleying into the net off his left. Nicholas has no physical attributes on the floor or in the air, but will work hard. Has good balance, control, change of pace and can beat opponents on his own, or by using ball. In the last half hour he played good 1-2's round the box. On one occasion he ran past three defenders then played a 1-2 and should have scored. Delivers the ball well, sees reverse passes. Made a good run and pull back for McLeish who should have scored. Turns very quickly on the ball apart from his ability to dribble, he is nearly always on the end of a move. Always looking to get shots in and invariably hits the target. Very well balanced and chips good crosses when going to the line on the ball.

Note: Not only does he look for goals but can make goals as well. A very good footballer! Aberdeen Strachan made good runs at the Swiss defence on the ball in last half hour.'

Nicholas would move to Arsenal a month or two after this particular match signing for Manager Terry Neill in June 1983. It would cost Neill nearly three quarters of a million pounds sterling and the Arsenal fans hoped it would be a worthwhile investment with their team sitting at number 10 in the first division. He retired in 1996 carving out a name for himself as a football pundit on Sky Sports.

~~~~

Tony Coton: This player was a young 21 year old goalkeeper for Birmingham City and he had been with them for several years before Collins looked at him. The match was a local Derby between Birmingham and West Bromwich Albion and the result would be a 2–1 win for Birmingham. The date was November 6th, 1982 and six feet tall Coton weighed in at 11 stone 8 lbs.

Coton's right foot was not used but left foot very good, kicking off the floor half way and over as well as kicking from hands with long high volleys. His attitude to physical contact seemed to be that he was not afraid, but won't knock anybody over. He came out quickly to through balls and his reading of the game was fairly good. Irrespective of the above, he is a good player.

'This was a strange game. West Brom had one shot at goal in the first half and two corners, yet they led one nothing at the interval. Birmingham had 12 shots at goal in the same period. Whilst Coton had nothing to do in the first half, I felt he had a chance to save the West Brom goal from a near post (flicked on) in-swinging corner. He was in the centre of his goal when the ball was flicked on and headed in on the far post. I felt he could have got across quicker. In the second half he came for another in-swinger and was caught adrift. He caught a couple of high balls from the flanks well enough, but doesn't look the type to come and take them amongst a rack of players. His handling was generally good in the air and on the floor. Although not having much to do, his general game was fairly good. There is still doubt about him coming and winning crosses under pressure. He doesn't look aggressive enough when coming out. He looks as though he will be a line goalkeeper unless it is a question of confidence just coming into the first team. The doubt about him coming for crosses will not be proved until he has a lot to do. He should still be followed for progress and to be seen under pressure.'

So, Tony Coton would drop into the Collins 'view again later' file and continue his career in football until 2007/8. He did in fact get onto the Manchester United staff as goalkeeping coach until a knee injury put him out of action for good. He would then move on to become a successful and well known football agent.

Match Reports

Not only were reports on players filed away in the secret drawers of Tony's ever growing collection of data. This was of course in the 'days before computers' and reports were referenced and cross referenced in a series of files that Tony used to evaluate a team's chances in any particular confrontation. They also pointed toward a player's possible value to a team and more importantly, how long such a value could be maintained. There are many, many files still in existence, enough to fill another book completely. However, the following report on a match between Manchester United (MU) and Sheffield Wednesday (SW) which took place on the 15th of March, 1997 is indicative of the kind of detail entered into in the analysis of the match and the part that individual team members played in it. Collins was reporting on the fixture for Derby County at the time with this report in preparation for the upcoming game with Manchester United at Old Trafford on April 5th. The result of the game, perhaps due to some excellent match intelligence provided by Collins, would be a 3–2 win for Derby and watched by a crowd of more than fifty five thousand. The result of this particular reported match however was a win for Manchester United by 2 goals to 0 and some memorable names were playing that day such as Beckham, Giggs, Cantona and Schmeichel. Beckham was a fit 21 year old who had been playing first team football with United since 1994 but was not yet really recognised as the world class footballer he would go on to be under the watchful eye of Alex Ferguson.

Attached to the match reports compiled by Collins were diagrams of match play and positioning that would be used in training and tactical study meetings. The report below provides for a star line-up of Beckham, Giggs, Cantona and Cole, the 'dream team' selection of the day and suitable comment is provided by the 'Master Spy' in frightening detail. The tactical diagram examples included show corner kicks taken by both Beckham and Giggs and how Tony Collins saw the line-up and subsequent movement of players on the pitch. This is a great example of Collins reporting style and eye for player positioning on the field of play.

Manchester United Line Up (4-3-1-2)

Schmeichel

G. Neville	May		Pallister	Irwin
	Beckham	Butt	Giggs	
		Cantona		
	Solskjaer		Cole	

Subs: P. Neville, Cruyff, Poborsky, Van Der Gouw and Scholes.
Conditions: Fine drizzle all afternoon.
Pitch: Good condition, fast surface.

In the first half of this game, SW had as much of the ball as MU. SW paid for two missed chances by striker Hirst before United scored.

United took the lead after 20 minutes through Cole. Giggs, who played tucked in a lot, moved the ball to Cantona facing him in the inside left position and ran for a return, but Cantona just checked and touched the ball on to Cole for a third man run to score. SW still had a lot of the ball, bringing both their full backs into play but only after making good space. They often delayed passes and finished up making too many before breaking down. SW had plenty of the ball in this first half, but through their own indecision they allowed MU to retrieve situations and break them down. Poborsky came on for Cole after 25 minutes. In the second half, Poborsky played a little wider on the right. Although United broke quickly and always looked possible scorers, they were still tentative at the back until they scored the second goal. This came from when Giggs checked back to his right foot to cross waist high to Cantona who cleverly helped the ball on to Solskjaer who in turn helped the ball onto Poborsky to score. After this goal MU looked as if they could have scored another two goals at least. Although they (MU) have other very good players, Cantona was behind most of their dangerous attacks. His craft and final balls were better than the others and we (Derby) must attempt to stifle him. SW allowed him too much freedom without paying him particular attention.

Pattern of Play: The MU starting formation of 4-3-1-2 had a flat back four that played fairly close together. However, this meant the full backs were left uncovered at times. Goal keeper Schmeichel generally kicked long off Solskjaer and Cantona. Solskjaer was generally running off to Cantona. The middle three played close most of the time with Butt sitting in on Beckham and Giggs tucked in alongside him. Giggs broke out wide at times, often more than Beckham which left MU short of width on the right. This seemed to take a bit away from Beckham's game because he seldom pulled very wide and generally hit early crosses through the box, which looked dangerous at times. However, it did help Cantona by giving him another open area to be able to drift into. The back four pushed out once the ball was cleared, but never came out a long way. They seemed to be afraid of runs in behind them. Pallister did not look properly fit and showed a lack of mobility when he had to turn. Beckham seldom checked out to free his full back. Right back Neville generally played to Solskjaer moving out to the flank off to Cantona and checking out deep.

On the left Giggs freed Irwin and when Irwin was bringing the ball out again, Solskjaer moved out unless Cantona checked out. If that happened then Cantona would play Giggs down the left. Giggs came through the inside left position a lot with Irwin supporting but seldom going all the way. When Poborsky came on for Cole he only played central striker for a short while, eventually moving more to the right flank with Cantona but still deeper than Solskjaer. Solskjaer did most of the front running showing good pace and change of pace (he cheats often by tugging and pulling at opponents) and some SW defenders were beaten by biting at him too early and not giving themselves a chance. Cantona did not do much running, but moved off opponents to join things up or play his team mates through. Although admittedly MU have more than a few good players, most of the telling balls in this match came from Cantona. Their most dangerous moves came from the left via Giggs and Cantona. They were not particularly good in the air up front so generally looked for a way to play through opponents. Although Poborsky scored a goal, he likes to run with the ball and invariably this meant he was often caught in possession. In the first half they (MU) were often overrun in midfield by SW especially when Humphreys dropped deeper than the rest to receive, thereby enabling him to transfer the ball to one of his oncoming full backs leaving Giggs and Beckham tucked in and Butt filling the space between them.

Unfortunately they failed to make much of this advantage. It also allowed SW front men to check out off Pallister to free midfield men or play oncoming full backs themselves.

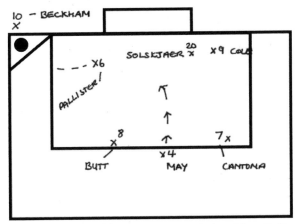

In-swinging corner on left taken by Beckham and played into Pallister on near post with Solskjaer, Cole, May and Cantona running off him.

The front men can play a big part in moving off their centre backs but they should move off them diagonally and half-on. If a player comes straight off Pallister full on, he'll go through him. May will be in on any 50/50 challenge but often backs off and gives unnecessary room when faced up. Moving them (MU) around should be exploited.

The Pallister, Irwin and Giggs side were more inclined to play their way out than the May, Neville, Beckham side where Beckham did not drop out to free full back Neville, forcing him on to longer balls to the front. So, it is better to leave May with the ball when the back four have possession. Whilst they all competed in the air at the back, only Pallister was able to dominate, so (we must) try to miss him out when crossing on corners. They (MU) play a lot of 1–2's round the box and it is fatal to follow the ball.

The Players:

Schmeichel 6'4 right sided – Goalkeeper: Kicking and handling excellent. Misjudged off cross but by and large governed his area well. Low balls through the box caused him most problems but read through balls well. Governed his defence and often kicked long to Cantona with Solskjaer running off him. Will start attacks with powerful throws given the chance. Generally a very good goalkeeper.

Back Four:

G. Neville, 5'10 right sided, right back - Good control, fairly good pace, fairly good in the air and tackled quite well. He was worried at times when taken on by SW player Blinker. He was supported but did not get down the flank much mainly because he had to hit longer balls to Cantona or Solskjaer. He was moving wide with Beckham and not dropping out to receive him. He covered well inside when opponents had the ball on the opposite flank.

May, 6'0 right sided, right/centre back – Average control, fairly good pace and fairly good in the air but never dominated. Enthusiastic but gets erratic under pressure. He's a battler who dives at times when losing patience. Will smash into opponent in 50/50 situations but sometimes allowed opponent to check out from him. Doesn't know whether to stay or close. He must be moved around and should not be left with the ball when they (MU) have possession.

Pallister, 6'4 right sided, left/centre back – Good control. Not quick off the mark but builds up to a reasonable pace. He lacks pace on turn and did not look properly fit. Good in the air. Recovery was slow. Will go right through a player if they move off him slowly but if they take him in first, then they need to check out or peel off for balls up alongside and that will give him problems. Try to miss him out on crosses.

Irwin, 5'8 right sided, left back – He can play off his left. Good control, average pace and not good in the air. Likes to use the ball and supports well. Covered well in when opponents had the ball on the opposite flank. Not a strong tackler but contains well. He will move down the flank if Giggs stays inside, but in this game it was mainly to join up. He likes to play his way out from the back.

This unit played close together covering each other. SW had them (MU) stretched early on and after not taking advantage of two chances, held the final ball too long allowing MU time to retrieve the situation. They pushed out once the ball was cleared but not too far.

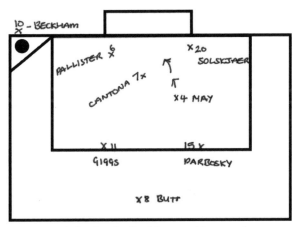

In-swinging corner on left taken by Beckham and long to far post towards May and Solskjaer, with Cantona and Pallister prepared for ball to be knocked down and across.

Whether they wanted to protect Pallister or not, I don't know because he was very slow in turning. There must be movement off these (MU) centre backs but it must be done sharply. With May, a player can move off him most times and with Pallister a player will have to try to take him inside first before checking out the free midfield players or full backs, or to peel off him for balls up alongside. Both full backs were always on to be brought into play. Try to miss Pallister out on crosses, free kicks and corners.

Midfield:

Beckham, 5'9 right sided, right midfield – Good control, average pace. Average in the air. He played tucked in and seldom broke wide leaving them (MU) without real width on the right. He generally hit early crosses through the box when pulling a little wide but not right out on the flank. This seemed to take a bit away from his game. He didn't drop out to release his right back. Possesses a very good shot ability but was seldom in a position to get shots in and had nobody to lend the ball out to until Paborsky came on for Cole who was injured after 25 minutes. He had a lot of running to do early in the game being pulled out by SW left back.

Butt, 5'9 right sided, right midfield – Good control and average pace. He is a strong, energy player who tackles hard. Predictable use and fairly strong in the air. He is a strong competitor.

Giggs, 5.10 left sided, left midfield – Very good control and excellent pace but average in the air. Played tucked in and only breaking wide occasionally. He dropped out to release left back Irwin and broke very quickly from deep positions. He joined up well with Cantona. Final balls at times let him down but at least he turns defenders. Recovers and covers ground well but not a strong tackler.

In the first 25 minutes when Cole and Solskjaer played together up front with Cantona behind them, this midfield unit was made to chase the ball by SW. Playing close together they were outnumbered with SW making five in midfield by dropping a midfield player deep from MU three and continually changing the play bringing a full back down the flank and Cantona not doing much chasing. This changed slightly when Cole went off injured with Paborsky coming on and eventually playing wide on the right after starting in the striking position. SW still had room in this area but not as much as before and their margin of error was cut down with cross-field balls to their full backs. The left side was MU's most dangerous via Giggs joining up with Cantona. On the right Paborsky ran into a lot of trouble on the ball.

Front Men:

Cantona, 6'1 right sided, number 7 and deep off front two – Excellent control with good touch and vision. Average pace, but quick off the mark and good change of pace. The instigator of most of their (MU) dangerous moves. He had his rests. Only played in short bursts but with the midfield playing without width, it gave him the freedom to go where he liked with everyone else filling in any space left by him. He moved to flanks or just checked out deeper to receive. He made both goals. The first as a 1-2 off Giggs where facing his own goal he went to play a return but checked the ball and played it narrower for Cole to score. The second goal came from Giggs checking back on the left to cross to Cantona off his right at waist-high for him to then quickly touch the ball on to Solskjaer to again produce a further touch on to Paborsky. Most of the danger came from this left side. He must be marked man for man or picked up thirty yards from the goal when they (MU) have possession, depending on who can do the job.

Cole, 5'11 right sided, striker – Good control once in possession but first touch not always good. Very good pace and although he could have scored more goals is very dangerous round the box. He made a third man run to score off Cantona through ball. He needs the ball in front of him and is not good facing his own goal. Don't get too close where he can run off your shoulder. He came off after 25 minutes.

Paborsky, 5.8 right sided, striker – Came on for Cole in striking position but pushed too wide on right later. Good control and reasonable pace and likes to run with the ball. He will give an opponent a chance if they don't dive at him and he overdoes it on the ball.

Solskjaer, 5'11 right sided, striker – Has very good control and a deceptive change of pace. He played up front alone after Cole went off and worked the width of the pitch. Pulled wide at times to give full backs an outlet. He made very good runs off the shoulders of defenders. His finishing is good, he works hard and links up well with others. He needed to be picked up when Cantona had possession. He cheats by leaning in and tugging at defenders. Don't get intimidated by his niggling because he changes pace very well. He's a very confident front runner.

Conclusion:

This (MU) is obviously a very good side. They get a lot of players round the ball in and out of possession. Cantona must be given consideration. He only played in bursts but the problem was that SW gave him too much freedom. The Irvin, Giggs, Cantona tie-up was their (MU) most dangerous link showing pace and guile. When in possession, the ball should be moved out of defence early. If we (Derby) cart the ball we will be in trouble. SW pulled their midfield around by popping the ball about and having one midfield player deep as an outlet because they like to crowd the ball area.

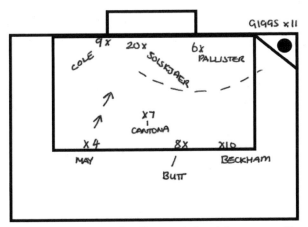

In-swinging corner on right taken by Giggs and aimed for centre of box with May and Cantona moving in late.

Our (Derby) front men can do a good job in freeing the midfield men or flanks by checking out off May and Pallister. With Pallister a player may have to feint to go inside him or go inside before checking out to receive or peel off for balls up alongside. If a player must come straight off him he'll go through them. He is slow on the turn. Try to miss him out on crosses. If the ball is moved around early, then good movement by the front men could cause them (MU) problems. Don't follow the ball in 1-2s around the box. If a player follows the ball it could prove fatal. They (MU) were not particularly good in the air up front and generally looking to play through opponents. May can be left with the ball but Pallister must be picked up on corners and free kicks.

It's interesting to note that in the May of 1997, only a few weeks after the date of this match report, Cantona would retire and leave the number seven shirt vacant. David Beckham would take this number, leaving his number ten shirt for the incoming Teddy Sheringham. So, at that point in the history of Manchester United, the Beckham legend, tied to the number seven shirt was really born. This was a number that had been worn by George Best and Bryan Robson in the past as well as Cantona and would go on to be worn by Cristiano Ronaldo.

Attached to the match reports compiled by Collins were diagrams of match play and positioning that would be used in training and tactical study meetings. The tactical diagrams included show corner kicks taken by Beckham and Giggs and how Tony Collins saw the line-up and subsequent movement of players on the pitch.

1	2	3	4	5	6	7	8	9	10
11	12	13	14	15	16	17	18	19	20
21	22	23	24	25	26	27	28	29	30
31	32	33	34	35	36	37	38	39	40
41	42	43	44	45	46	47	48	49	50
51	52	53	54	55	56	57	58	59	60
61	62	63	64	65	66	67	68	69	70
71	72	73	74	75	76	77	78	79	80
81	82	83	84	85	86	87	88	89	90
91	92	93	94	95	96	97	98	99	100
101	102	103	104	105	106	107	108	109	110
111	112	113	114	115	116	117	118	119	120
121	122	123	124	125	126	127	128	129	130
131	132	133	134	135	136	137	138	139	140
141	142	143	144	145	146	147	148	149	150
151	152	153	154	155	156	157	158	159	160
161	162	163	164	165	166	167	168	169	170
171	172	173	174	175	176	177	178	179	180
181	182	183	184	185	186	187	188	189	190
191	192	193	194	195	196	197	198	199	200
201	202	203	204	205	206	207	208	209	210
211	212	213	214	215	216	217	218	219	220
221	222	223	224	225	226	227	228	229	230
231	232	233	234	235	236	237	238	239	240
241	242	243	244	245	246	247	248	249	250
251	252	253	254	255	256	257	258	259	260
261	262	263	264	265	266	267	268	269	270
271	272	273	274	275	276	277	278	279	280
281	282	283	284	285	286	287	288	289	290
291	292	293	294	295	296	297	298	299	300
301	302	303	304	305	306	307	308	309	310
311	312	313	314	315	316	317	318	319	320
321	322	323	324	325	326	327	328	329	330
331	332	333	334	335	336	337	338	339	340
341	342	343	344	345	346	347	348	349	350
351	352	353	354	355	356	357	358	359	360
361	362	363	364	365	366	367	368	369	370
371	372	373	374	375	376	377	378	379	380
381	382	383	384	385	386	387	388	389	390
391	392	393	394	395	396	397	398	399	400